PILLARS
The Ten Commandments...Still Standing After Centuries of Change

Randel Everett

Pillars: The Ten Commandments... Still Standing After Centuries of Change

by Randel Everett

Published by Austin Brothers Publishing
Keller, Texas
www.austinbrotherspublishing.com

Copyright © 2012
Randel Everett
All rights reserved
ISBN 978-0-9853263-3-3

Scripture quotations, unless otherwise noted, are from the New American Standard Bible. Copyright 1998 by The International Bible Society. Used by permission.

All Rights Reserved. No part of this book may be reproduced in any form without permission in writing from the publisher, except in the case of brief quotations embodied in critical reviews or articles.

To my wife Sheila,
who is a pillar of
faith and encouragement to me.

Contents

Prologue	1
Holding on to Absolutes in a Nihilistic World	4
The Foundational Commandment	17
Substituting Ritual for Reality	26
Reverence for God's Name	38
Celebrating the Lord's Day	47
Worthy of Respect	57
The Sanctity of Life	70
Being Moral in an Immoral World	83
Taking or Giving?	97
Speaking the Truth in Love	105
Desiring the Best	114
Epilogue	121

Prologue

Pillars. Columns of antiquity still standing after centuries of change are symbols of hope for a world in a state of flux. The Arab Spring illustrates the restlessness of masses of individuals who are now capable of sharing their frustrations through the social media. Not even repressive governments can suppress them. Is there hope for people to live together in freedom and harmony?

Rapidly changing technology and the frustration with American nihilism have brought about a disappointing search for permanence and direction. Some seek comfort by an attempt to turn the clock back to a safer period of time when issues did not appear so complex. Others still await the discovery of enlightened inquiry, believing that the source for meaningful existence is yet to be found.

Not even history is sacred. Each culture seeks to read into the past whatever gives credence to its own values. Political correctness becomes more important to some university curricula than objective data.

A vacuum of leadership has developed as some government officials become motivated by public opinion polls instead of ideology. Public schools struggle with the teaching of values without offending the students' religious heritage. Nations where freedom of speech is allowed wrestle with the distinction between tolerance and obscenity. Yet there is a commonly held persuasion that societies must have moral boundaries or utter chaos will occur.

Whether we like it or not, a crisis of morality has dawned upon the twenty-first century. The issues of life are real: AIDS, abortion, war, racism, greed, definition of marriage, and issues of sexuality. Can we rummage around in the rubble of fallen cultures and find a moral code still standing? Yes! Like the pillars of the Parthenon amidst the debris, there on Mount Sinai we see the Ten Commandments. They are still calling us to a reverence for the Eternal God of order and purpose...challenging us to a respect for the rights and needs of others...and pointing us to a Savior who has come to write the Law on our hearts.

The Ten Commandments of God are relevant. The Ephesians' philosopher, Heraclitus, 560 B.C., said that the whole world is in a state of change. You can't step twice into the same river. Once you step again, it is a new river. Yet, if the world is so chaotic, what is the constant that controls it and keeps it from spinning off into oblivion? The Logos, Heraclitus said, is guiding the world and bringing it order.

The Commandments were written by the hand of the Logos. Almost seven centuries after Heraclitus, in the same city of Ephesus, the apostle John wrote, *"And the Word (Logos) became flesh, and dwelt among us, and we saw His glory, glory as of the only begotten from the Father, full of grace and truth"* (John 1:14). As we re-examine the Commandments, keep in mind that the One who has given them is the One who enables us to keep them. The One who created us has given us principles of life, not of bondage.

Holding on to Absolutes in a Nihilistic World

Travel and social media have created a world where events in a remote community are immediately known globally. The Arab Spring was a revolution fueled by social media. Powerful governments were no match for the hordes of people emboldened by the realization that they were not alone.

Individuals no longer wait for news to come to them from large media outlets. Stories go viral. It has become more difficult for governments or religions to keep their constituency isolated from other values and opinions.

Nihilism is a predictable outcome of this pluralistic multicultural world. How can anyone say they have absolute truth? Is any religion, or world view, better than another? All things have become relative. Tolerance has become the new god.

I sometimes have the feeling that "everything nailed down is coming loose... The line occurs in *Green Pastures,* a play by Marc Connelly that has found a permanent niche in the history of American drama. Looking down from heaven on earth's confusion and turmoil, Gabriel noted sadly: 'Everything nailed down is coming loose.'"[1]

Like the world of ancient Israel, our world is in cultural chaos. When the Israelites needed guidance to combat the ethical disorder of their day, God gave a set of Laws, simple and direct. They are known now as the Ten Commandments. Is it possible that ten ancient laws can save our present society from its own destruction?

What an incredible ethical and moral crisis faces the world! Society may not see the situation as primarily theological. However, like General Douglas MacArthur assessed the post-World War II situation in Japan, the basis of every cultural crisis is ultimately theological. Ours is an ethical crisis of gargantuan proportions, which pervades every aspect of our society.

Leaders in business, politics, sports, and even religion have been linked to scandals raging from fraud to immorality to physical abuses. A few decades ago homosexual activity was treated as a psychological disorder, yet today anyone who even questions same sex partnerships is viewed as out of step with the new morality and seen as narrow and judgmental. The President and Vice President have become advocates for same sex marriage. At first the

---

[1] Marshall W. Fishwick, *Saturday Review*, June 29,1963, page 11.

argument was compassion, a desire to live in a nation where anyone can love whomever he/she chooses. Then the argument became judgmental, gays have the same *right* as heterosexuals to marry.

When cultural attitudes become the litmus test for morality, where are the lines drawn? If we are a nation where we are free to love whomever we choose should we apologize to Warren Jeffs, the self-proclaimed prophet and leader of the YFZ ranch in El Dorado, Texas, who is in prison? He directed his flock, The Fundamentalist Church of Latter Day Saints (FLDS), and arranged celestial marriages saying that no man can attain the Kingdom of God with fewer than three wives. In a world without absolutes, which of us can say that polygamy is wrong or why would one restrict a forty year-old man from marrying a thirteen year-old girl?

Most boomers can remember when it was scandalous for a child to be born out of wedlock. Yet today almost half of the babies born in our country are born from a mother who is unmarried. When prominent individuals like Tim Tebow represent themselves as Christians who vow celibacy until marriage they are treated as the brunt of Hollywood humor.

Surely the time has come when we must apply moral standards and exercise the self-discipline so sadly lacking in our society. William Barclay, the Scottish Bible teacher and author, wrote in *The Ten Commandments for Today* about the moral crisis and the lack of discipline in a way that characterizes our own generation.

> *"In the name of freedom this generation resents discipline; it does not like commandments of any kind. Least of all does it like commandments which are also prohibitions. It does not like to be told not to do anything. Unlimited freedom and unrestricted permission to experiment are the contemporary demands.*
>
> *In a situation such as this, liberty can very easily become license, and the right to experiment can become the right to wreck one's own life and the lives of others. It is therefore well and good that this generation should be confronted with the uncompromising demands of the Ten Commandments. It may not accept them, but it should certainly face them."*[2]

Because every generation has needed rules to live by, there were written codes of ethics even before the time of Moses. As early as 1692 B.C. the Babylonians possessed the Code of Hammurabi, which is similar to the Jewish Ten Commandments. Some historians say that this Babylonian Code of Hammurabi is the source of the Ten Commandments and that the Israelites just gathered together this ethical and moral code from other nations. But this understanding overlooks the meaning of Exodus 20:1: *"Then God spoke all these words..."* There were, no doubt, laws written at different times for other societies.

---

2 William Barclay, *The Ten Commandments for Today*, Harper and Row, 1973, page 9.

But the Ten Commandments are commandments that were given to us by the Lord God Himself.

Someone will ask, "If Moses lived about 1500 B.C., were there no ethics, no morality, before the giving of the Ten Commandments?" Of course there were. What God spoke to them on the mountain was already a part of the fabric of their lives, in the same way that the laws of physics were a part of their lives.

When Cain killed Abel, long before the giving of the Ten Commandments, Cain knew that it was wrong to kill his brother. When Abraham lied about Sarah, his wife, and called her his sister so that he might be protected in a foreign country, he knew that lying was wrong, even though God had not specifically said, *"Thou shall not bear false witness."* When Rachel stole from her father Laban on the way to the land of Canaan, she knew that stealing was not right. And when Joseph was tempted by Potiphar's wife, he knew that the thing she was asking him to do would be displeasing in the sight of God. Even though there had never been a revealed, written code from God, there was already a sense of what is right and wrong in the hearts and minds of humanity.

Even today we do many things that are wrong in spite of the fact that in our hearts we know already that they are bad. One example is premarital sex. In our local school district more than 150 students are pregnant. I hate to imagine how many students are sexually active. Adelle

M. Banks wrote in an article for Religion News Service, "Eighty percent of young evangelicals have engaged in premarital sex, according to a new video from the National Association of Evangelicals. And almost a third of evangelicals' unplanned pregnancies end in abortion."[3]

We know it is wrong; even though a school nurse puts contraceptives in a girl's hands; even though her mother puts her on birth control pills; even though her friends say, "Everyone is doing it." Even though her boyfriend says, "Prove your love for me." It is wrong. It has always been wrong. It will always be wrong and in our heart we know it is not right.

Premarital sex is violation of another person. It is a violation of the eternal Law of the universe and the holiness of God. It is a terrible thing to risk the consequences— AIDS, venereal diseases, and destruction of the trust that is the foundation of marriage.

So if the Law of God is written into our hearts, what is the need for the commandments? What was God's purpose in giving the Law to Moses on Mount Sinai?

One reason was to enable us to see the holiness of God. When Jesus spoke of about the Ten Commandments in the Sermon on the Mount, He spoke with a profound understanding about who God is, theologically as well as historically. God, who heard the Israelites cry out when they were captive in Egypt, and responded to those cries,

---
3 Adelle M. Banks, "Evangelicals say it's time for frank talk about sex," *Baptist Standard*, May 14, 2012, page 14.

gave the Law out of His attentiveness and out of love for His creation. Jesus recognized that God's purpose in the Law was to give us a way, through obedience, to recognize that He is both holy and righteous.

Just as the commandments show me that God is righteous and holy, they show me my utter sinfulness and unrighteousness. Just as God is light, I am darkness. Just as God is holy, I am unholy.

When the apostle Paul was explaining the purpose of the Law (Romans 3:19-21), he wrote that the Law brings to us the knowledge of sin. God spelled it out so that, as we look in the mirror of God's holiness, we'll see that we are sinful, that we are immoral.

We, like Isaiah, fall on our faces when we see the righteousness of God and say, *"Woe is me...I am a man of unclean lips, and I live among a people of unclean lips..."* (Isaiah 6:5).

While the giving of the Law was to show us the holiness of God and the sinfulness of man, it was also given to restrain behavior that was unacceptable. These commandments serve to keep order, to restrain individuals who cause disorder, to help the world take a giant step away from cultural chaos. The nation of Israel needed to have laws that would say a certain kind of behavior would not be tolerated and that another kind of behavior would be acceptable. If such a need was evident then, how much more is it evident today!

Certainly one of the greatest purposes of the Law is stated in Galatians 3:24, where Paul writes that the Law has been given to me as a tutor, to lead me to God, to lead me to Christ. It is through the Law that I realize that I need a Messiah. When I hold myself up to the Law of God, when I compare my conduct and the state of my heart to the revealed Law of God, I realize not only that I've sinned but that I have a propensity for sinning, that I—in my own flesh—will continue to go on in the direction of sinfulness. Therefore, I need a Savior. As we all do. We need an intervention from God. We need God to come and do in us, through us, and for us what we cannot do for ourselves. Humankind didn't need just to be stronger in its discipline. It needed the intervention of the Holy Spirit, who would write the Law—not externally on stone like that given to the Israelites but in the heart and mind of each of us.

Recognizing the various purposes of the Ten Commandments, we can begin to think about their characteristics. First of all, they are absolute. They are not ten suggestions! The phrasing of each says strongly, "You shall!" or "You shall not!" There is no ambiguity.

Second, the commandments are personal. This personal element is not readily apparent because in English there is no difference in the second person singular and second person plural. In the Hebrew text, however, the word "you" is singular in each of the Ten Commandments. They are written to and for *you*, to and for *me*. The fact is they are addressed to each person individually, and not to Israel generally. This emphasizes the importance of internal motivation in obedience rather than corporate pressure or external coercion.

Looking more clearly at the commandments, we can analyze the directions of their reach! The first four are vertical, requiring reverence for God. The last six are horizontal, demanding respect for humanity. Our Western society's laws and culture have derived more from these Ten Commandments than from any other document of antiquity. A society without boundaries is anarchy, so there must be a labeling of those things that are right and those that are wrong. As a society and as individuals we must be clear about them lest we destroy each other. A study of the Ten Commandments helps us set the necessary boundaries.

Eight of the commandments are negative. For that reason alone some say, "They are not valid for us today. They are an expression of a negative faith."

I rediscovered the book entitled *Smoke on the Mountain* by Joy Davidman. (C. S. Lewis wrote a moving account of their marriage and her death from cancer in his book *A Grief Observed*.) In her provocative and profoundly thoughtful book Ms. Davidman tells the story about a missionary who was in a dark corner of Africa where the men filed their teeth to sharp points. The missionary worked hard trying to lead a very old native chief to the Lord. It was difficult for this African, steeped in the ways of his country, to understand what Christianity was all about, especially since the missionary's version of Christianity leaned heavily on thou-shall-not's. But the man listened patiently.

"I don't understand," he said at last. "You tell me that I must not take my neighbor's wife." "That is right," said the missionary. "Or his ivory, or his oxen." "Quite right." "And I must not dance the war dance and then ambush him on the trail and kill him." "Absolutely right!" "But I can't do any of these things!" said the chief regretfully. "I'm too old. To be old and to be a Christian, they are the same thing!"[4]

Many people think of Christianity in the same way, as a compilation of "do's and don't's," useful only for those who are too old to have any fun.

Some of those same folks think preachers operate like the irritable woman who said, "Find out what the children are doing and tell them to stop it."[5]

J. I. Packer, the English writer, said that we need to study the Ten Commandments to understand love. Law and love form the axis of true morality because Law without love becomes more interested in principle than in people. And yet love is blind, and so the Law becomes the eyes of love.[6]

---

4 Joy Davidman, *Smoke on the Mountain*, Westminster Press, 1976, page 13.
5 Davidman, page 14.
6 J. I. Packer, *The Ten Commandments*, Tyndale House, 1986, page 24.

There is much criticism, some of it valid, about Christianity being a legalistic faith. The criticizers say that we, like the African missionary, place more emphasis on negatives than on the positive aspects of our faith. They say, "Since we are Christians, we are no longer living under Law. We are living under grace."

On the contrary, in the Old Testament we see law and grace, and in the New Testament we see law and grace. Jesus' teachings were based on and related to the Law. He did not in any way indicate to us that His coming released us from the Law. In the Sermon on the Mount, which is a fuller interpretation of the Ten Commandments, Jesus said, *"Do not think that I came to abolish the Law or the Prophets; I did not come to abolish, but to fulfill"* (Matthew 5:17). As a matter of fact, instead of doing away with it, He extended the implications of the Law.

For example, in the Ten Commandments it is written, *"You shall not murder."* But Jesus said, *"...But I say to you that everyone who is angry with his brother shall be guilty before the court; and whoever shall say to his brother, 'you good-for-nothing,' shall be guilty before the supreme court; and whoever says, 'You fool,' shall be guilty enough to go into the fiery hell"* (Matthew 5:22).

We find in the Ten Commandments, *"You shall not commit adultery."* But Jesus said, *"...but I say to you, that everyone who looks at a woman with lust for her has already committed adultery with her in his heart"* (Matthew 5:28).

In the Ten Commandments we read, "*You shall not bear false witness.*" But Jesus said, "*But I say to you, make no oath at all, either by heaven, for it is the throne of God, or by the earth, for it is the footstool of His feet, or by Jerusalem, for it is the city of the Great King. Nor shall you make an oath by your head, for you cannot make one hair white or black. But let your statement be 'Yes, yes' or 'No, no'; anything beyond these is of evil*" (Matthew 5:34-37).

It is evident from these New Testament teachings that Jesus did not come to abolish or to annul the Ten Commandments. He came to extend and refine and help us to understand the intent of the commandments. But more than that, Jesus came to fulfill the Law. He Himself said, "*I did not come to abolish, but to fulfill*" (Matthew 5:17).

The Apostle Paul, writing in Romans 8:3-4, wrote that what the Law could not do, weak as it was in the flesh, God did by sending His Only Begotten Son. From the Scriptures we come to understand that the Law is a container, a vessel. While a vessel by itself may have some value as a piece of art, it becomes truly valuable when it is filled full of substance. And just as the Law is the container, Jesus came to fill it full with Himself. The One who has given these ten basic laws is the One who enables us to keep them.

The nation of Israel was in a covenant relationship with God. It did not matter what Egypt or other nations believed about morality, God spoke very clearly to the children of Abraham about what He expected of them. The United

States was founded on Judeo-Christian morality. For most of its history the law of the land has been somewhat compatible with the law of Scripture. As citizens of a free nation we must do everything we can to preserve these laws. However, like Israel, the Church is in a covenant relationship with God. Regardless of cultural shifts or opinions, God has spoken clearly about His expectations of His people.

The Foundational Commandment

You shall have no other gods before Me.

Exodus 20:3

When Moses delivered to his people the word of God in the form of the Ten Commandments, his preface was, "*God spoke all these words...*" Then he relayed them in an order we are to assume was God's own order. While we cannot judge that any one commandment is more important than another, there must have been a reason for the placement of the first commandment: "*You shall have no other gods before Me.*"

Not knowing the reason, we may dismiss this command as the one we are least likely to violate, for who among us worships Ra, the sun god? Who among us has an altar to Baal in our homes?

In Moses' day, however, each small segment of the world's cultures had its own god. The Israelites were just beginning to understand what it meant to worship the true God of the Universe when the creator God spoke and said, *"You shall have no other gods before Me."* The preposition "before" is, in many Bible notes, also translated "besides." The text is not referring to an establishment of priorities among the gods. It means "You shall not have any gods in addition to Me." Very literally it could be translated "You shall have no other gods in my presence." It is not that the Lord is god over all the other gods. It is that "the Lord is the one God."

When the Hebrew men pray early in the morning and late in the evening, they recite the Shema (Deuteronomy 6:4). They come together and say, *"Hear, O Israel! The Lord is our God, the Lord is one!"* Not one among many, not the greatest of several, but one God, the creator God of all heaven and earth. Even though we may accept that concept without question today, it was revolutionary at Mount Sinai.

We understand that He is *exclusively God.* This understanding about God is the major difference between the other moral codes and the Ten Commandments that Moses received. The other codes are simply moral statements. Nothing is wrong with them, but the Ten Commandments not only make moral statements, they include definitive implications about the God of the Universe.

It is important to get the idea of God right because we inevitably become like the god we worship. If we worship an immoral god, we become lewd in our behavior. If we worship an arbitrary, hostile god, we become angry and antagonistic. If our god is a legalistic, demanding and harsh god we also become legalistic, demanding and harsh. If we worship a sentimental god, then we become emotional in our approach to god and to others in life. We become like the god we worship.

Moses knew that Egyptians worshipped Ra, the Philistines worshipped Dagon, and the Sidonians worshipped Baal. Is it any wonder then that he asked God, "What is your name? What do I tell the people when I tell them that God has sent me?"

In response God gave us His name, "I AM." Very literally His name could be interpreted "I will continuously be who I have always been!" The name *Yahweh* is probably our best description of the "I AM" name for God.

He also said, "I am the God of Abraham, Isaac and Jacob." The people needed to be reminded that our God is a covenant God. In all of His holiness and His righteousness, God entered into a covenant with Abraham and his descendants so that all the peoples of the world may be blessed through them. When God says, "*I am the Lord your God*" (Exodus 20:2), He is saying, "I am a covenant God. I am the Yahweh God who spoke to Moses. I am a personal God. I am a redeemer God."

Before the Lord met with Israel on Mount Sinai, the people had been slaves in Egypt. With a very dramatic hand God had prepared Moses and Aaron. With their leadership and with the help of the ten plagues God had led them out of a land of captivity, where they had lived for over four hundred years. He brought them out into the wilderness on the way to their new home, the Promised Land. With great drama God had parted the Red Sea, and the pursuing Egyptian army was killed.

The Lord had already earned their respect and their trust. God was not just someone who spoke to them in the midst of the desert. God was the One who had shown His relationship very deliberately; through a covenant with Abraham through the preservation of the Israelites, through Joseph, through the ten plagues, and through the mighty hand of Moses. And now God said, "In light of the fact that I have entered into this covenant relationship of grace and redemption with you, let me speak to you about the kind of people you ought to be."

We see the Covenant/Redeemer God in action today, thousands of years after Sinai. The same God who gave us the Ten Commandments has made provision for the redemption of sinners, for those who in repentance cast themselves upon His grace, for those of us who are in need of daily sustenance. He is the Redeemer God whom we may approach with the needs of our desperate hearts. How many times, like St. Paul, have we said, "*Wretched man that I am! Who will set me free from the body of this death*

(Romans 7:24)?" Can we then say, also like Paul, *"Thanks be to God through Jesus Christ our Lord* (Romans 7:25)?"

The same God that brought the Israelites out of the land of captivity is here to release us from the bondage of our own sinfulness. Our initial step must be to heed the first commandment and make Yahweh central to our lives, worshipping only Him.

Today our gods may not be only religious idols but we have cultural ideals to which we give our allegiance, such as materialism, recreation, vocations or pleasure. We may place our faith in morality, religion, science, politics or human ingenuity. Some attempt to escape the cares of this world through obsessions with social media, television, drugs or alcohol.

In addition, there are other more "noble" and incredibly subtle gods that we worship which are truly seductive and often insinuate themselves between the Christian and God. Honorable causes, such as world peace or the environment can demand our primary allegiance. Success can become our god, even among pastors who place church growth above a personal, absolute reverence of the Lord God. While we must work for peace, a clean environment, equality for all, and evangelism, no effort can claim our devotion due to the One True God.

In Joy Davidman's book, *Smoke on the Mountain*, she identifies the gods of Sex, the State, Science, and Society.[7] Almost anything we buy is regularly promoted, at times

---
7 Davidman, page 26.

subtly, sometimes blatantly, by the use of sex. The psychological masterminds of Madison Avenue tell us their products, whether automobiles or soap or jeans or beer, will bring sexual fulfillment. When we use their product we will discover life, real life. If we had a visitor from ancient Egypt, I can imagine that he would look around and say, "They worship a sex god."

This abuse of sex is rife with implications. Compare it to the act of spitting on the altar in God's house. Such an act would be a desecration of the temple of God. Yet the Bible says that our bodies are temples of the Holy Spirit (1 Corinthians 6:19-20), so when we commit sexual defilement we are committing a sin that is far greater than spitting on an altar.

Another god worshipped today is the great god of Science. In science, some say, we find all the answers. If we will just stay longer in the lab and appropriate more funds for research, then we'll be able to find the solutions to all the crises and all the problems of life. But the more we discover in the laboratory, the more we realize that the questions of life are still with us. The great questions are not scientific. They are moral and theological.

Some live as though the State were their god. It is "my country right or wrong." Many ethnic, religious, and nationalistic groups have segmented the world into hostile divisions, intolerant of each other and dedicated, at all costs, to preserving their land and their ideology. One astronaut looked back to the earth as he orbited and said he was impressed that he saw no boundaries.

There are also those whose god is Society. Believing like the ancient Romans, that "the safety of the peoples is the supreme law," they put more trust in sociology and psychiatry than in God.

Our nation has truly become a melting pot of religions. Even small communities have churches, synagogues, mosques and temples. While they offer a variety of cultural stories and traditions, they also confuse with diverse moral codes, diets and agendas. We live more in the Athens of Acts 17 than the Jerusalem world of Acts 2. If we preach the scripture as Peter did in Jerusalem, or refer to David and Joel, the people will ask whose scripture and will question who are David and Joel.

Organized religion has been shunned by a generation who has lost confidence in institutions. However we find in them a deep hunger for spiritual things and a longing for authenticity and community. They are often mosaic thinkers instead of linear and find absolutes confining, archaic and even repulsive. Some form their own gods, blending in a little Jesus, Mohammed, Gandhi and Oprah. It is strange for them to hear that the Lord our God is one god, or that Jesus is the only way to the Father.

Christ followers cannot have divided loyalties among several gods. In the scripture from Exodus the Lord says, *"You shall have no other gods before me."* We cannot have God and country, God and success, God and peace, God and prosperity. God said, "I am the Lord your God. You shall have no other gods before me." Later Joshua would say "...choose for yourselves today whom you will serve: whether the gods which your fathers served which were beyond the River, or the gods of the Amorites in whose land you are living; but as for me and my house, we will serve the Lord" (Joshua 24:15). On Mount Carmel Elijah said, "How long will you hesitate between two opinions? If the Lord is God, follow Him; but if Baal, follow him" (1 Kings 18:21).

Jesus said, "No one can serve two masters; for either he will hate the one and love the other, or he will be devoted to one and despise the other. You cannot serve God and wealth" (Matthew 6:24). The Lord is God and He will not share loyalty with another.

Tom Oden in *Two Worlds* summarizes the methods we use to choose our gods when he writes,

> *"Any finite good can become a potential idolatry. To be worshipped as a god, something must be sufficiently good to be plausibly regarded as the rightful center of one's valuing. Otherwise it is not even a decent candidate for idolatry. That which has no power to tempt us to worship it is not good enough to become a credible potential idolatry. If education were not a source of enormous good, it would not tempt us to make it a god. If one's motherland, regional identity or family tradition were not exceptionally meaningful, it would not tempt us to make it a center of value. But precisely because these things are of such inestimable value to us,*

they tempt us toward idolatry...One has a god when a finite value is worshipped and adored and viewed as that without which one cannot receive life joyfully."[8]

What is it in your life and mine that stands between us and the total lordship of Christ? Who is your god? To what do you give your ultimate allegiance? What is it that elicits your deepest feeling and your ultimate concern?

How we need to pray that the Holy Spirit would examine our hearts and our minds and reveal to us any purpose or any event, any ambition or any person that stands above God in our lives so that we might with unity and one voice say, "Hear, all of you; the Lord, He is God. The Lord, He is our God."

God must have placed this particular commandment at the top of the list because it is the pivotal commandment. It tells us without equivocation that our relationship to the God of the Universe is an exclusive one. It is the foundation for all the other commands. It is the means by which we can obey them all.

---

[8] Tom Oden, *Two Worlds*, Intervarsity Press, 1992.

Substituting Ritual for Reality

You shall not make for yourself an idol, or any likeness of what is in heaven above or on the earth beneath or in the water under the earth. You shall not worship them or serve them; for I, the Lord your God, am a jealous God, visiting the iniquity of the fathers on the children, on the third and fourth generations of those who hate Me, but showing lovingkindness to thousands, to those who love Me and keep My commandments.

Exodus 20:4-6

In a cartoon drawing of the front door of a church, there is the bulletin board announcing the day's sermon on the Ten Commandments. A man and his wife coming down the church steps have doubtless just heard the announced sermon. The man looks at his wife and says, "Well, at least I haven't made any graven images!"

Even if we may have broken other commandments, on this one, at least, we feel safe. We have not made any graven images. We do not have idols on our mantels at home. At first this commandment might seem irrelevant to us as twenty-first century Christians. But we must be careful not to forgive ourselves too quickly! Instead of its having no significance, we find that the second commandment is very important in our day. The first clue to its importance is its length. The second clue may be that it is second in the order of the Commandments, coming directly after a statement of exclusivity, that God alone is the Lord.

The prohibition against idol-making does not mean that in our minds there won't be attempts to construct a picture of what God looks like. Although my guess is that any imagined image is going to be wrong, I don't know how we cannot have mental images of God, for we are visual people. We learn by images. We remember by images. This commandment is not saying that we shouldn't have mental images of God.

As we study the history of the way God revealed Himself to His people, we know that the Israelites must have had pictures in their minds. Their religious festivals were filled with representations of how God met His chosen people and redeemed them. There is no implication that mental images are wrong. Nor does the commandment say that art forms are forbidden. Some people understand this scripture to mean that art is wrong. They shun any kind of religious art, thinking the art form in itself is bad. However, the Old Testament describes the use of art in religious services. For example, the Tabernacle and the Temple of Solomon had images of cherubim, along with other kinds of art, some of it prescribed by the voice of God (Exodus 25:18).

Religious art can be very important to us. I was deeply moved by a painting that I observed in the Hermitage Museum in St. Petersburg, Russia. Before 1917 the Hermitage was a palace for the Imperial family and is now a magnificent museum, a truly fascinating place. In this Far Eastern country where religion had been outlawed for seventy-five years, a significant portion of the paintings had their roots in the Holy Scripture. Many of the Dutch Masters are displayed there, including Rembrandt's painting of *The Return of the Prodigal Son*. I sat before the painting for an extended period of time and reflected on it. I gained insights into the parable just by observing the way Rembrandt depicted the characters.

I shared this story with my church when I returned and one of our members mentioned a similar experience Henri Nouwen, the renowned Catholic theologian, had with the same painting. The friend referred me to his book entitled, *The Return of the Prodigal Son*,[9] where Nouwen shares the insights from this painting and how it deepened his understanding of both the parable and its insights to us in understanding the nature of God as Father. Sheila bought me a copy of the painting for my fiftieth birthday and it

---

9   Henri J. M. Nouwen, *The Return of the Prodigal Son*, Doubleday, 1994.

has a prominent place in my office where I see it every day.

Preachers use stories, artists use canvas, and musicians use instruments to communicate the powerful images of God. God used the biblical writers to communicate the Lord who is like a good shepherd, a loving father, and a king. Images are not wrong but they are incomplete. No single image can communicate the awesome nature of the true God.

If the second commandment is not a prohibition against art or against our attempts to picture God in our minds, then what does it say to us? It recognizes that deep in our hearts we desire to see God. We have a hunger to know Him.

We talk about God. We worship Him. We pray to Him. We sing praises to Him. Why would we not want to see His face? Moses asked to see God's face. On Mount Sinai Moses said to God, *"I pray You, show me see your glory"* (Exodus 33:18). God had spoken to him audibly, but Moses still wanted to see His glory. God then said, *"You cannot see My face, for no man can see Me and live!"* (Exodus 33:20).

The children of Israel, too, wanted a God they could see (Exodus 32:1). Even after they had experienced the very dramatic way that God had brought them out of Egypt, even when they knew that they were moving to the Promised Land, they wanted a God they could see. With Moses gone from them—although he was on the mountain receiving God's message for them—they longed for a visible and concrete manifestation.

> "Now when the people saw that Moses delayed to come down from the mountain, the people assembled about Aaron and said to him, 'Come, make us a god who will go before us; as for this Moses, the man who brought us up from the land of Egypt, we do not know what has become of him.' Aaron said to them, 'Tear off the gold rings which are in the ears of your wives, your sons, your daughters, and bring them to me.' Then all the people tore off the gold rings which were in their ears, and brought them to Aaron. He took this from their hand, and fashioned it with a graving tool and made it into a molten calf; and they said, 'This is your god, O Israel, who brought you up from the land of Egypt'" (Exodus 32:1-4).

I believe they thought they were making a visual representation of the god that had brought them out of Egypt. They were trying to put a god, Yahweh, into a piece of gold. They wanted a god they could see, but in doing so they substituted a graven image for the real thing.

An Old Testament story in the twenty-first chapter of Numbers illustrates yet another time when the Israelites made the same mistake. God, who was angry at them for their impatience in the wilderness before they entered the Promised Land, sent fiery serpents among the people. Later, when they repented of their impatience, God instructed Moses to make a sign to remind the people of

His power: a bronze serpent on a pole. After many years, however, the bronze pole became an object of worship for the people. Hezekiah had to break it into pieces, for *"the sons of Israel burned incense to it; and it was called Nehushtan"* (2 Kings 18:4).

What is the principle that we are taught through this commandment? Isn't it that we should not substitute replicas for relationships? We tend to be afraid of relationships in our twenty-first century culture. There are times, even in the midst of crowds of people who have similar backgrounds and interests, when we feel alone. Sometimes we do ridiculous things just to get the attention of others so they will acknowledge that we exist. Students "act out" in classrooms crying out for someone to notice them.

Yet as much as we want others to know us, there is a deep fear within us of entering into any kind of relationship. Many have turned to superficial friendships through Facebook where we can pretend to be something we are not and select what we want others to know about us. When we reach for something to hang on to, it is important that you and I beware of letting symbols or fantasies take the place of the reality of relationships in our lives.

William Barclay cites scriptures which point out the folly of idols. Man takes a piece of wood and with one small bit of it he makes a fire to warm himself; with another bit of it he makes a fire to cook his dinner; and with the third bit of it he makes a god (Isaiah 44:14-20). Barclay notes as well, the impracticality of idols: the idol is incapable of movement, fixed to one place as a scarecrow in a cucumber field (Jeremiah 10:3-5). Also, he wonders why we want to be burdened by our gods: When in the day of war a town is invaded, the citizens flee from it staggering under the weight of the idols, the gods, that they are carrying on their shoulders (Isaiah 46:1, 2, 7).[10]

Among things in our lives that become idols for us are things meant to bring us closer to God. This may be true even of things that are as important, helpful, and necessary as the Bible. People say, "The Bible is the Word of God. I believe every word in the Bible from the table of contents to the concordance." We wave it over our heads to emphasize our belief. We carry it proudly and sometimes ostentatiously. We give it a prominent place in our homes. Such reverence for the book, however, sometimes indicates more regard for the pages and binding than for the God whose Word it represents.

The same thing can happen with the sanctuary in which we worship. For a long time Baptists wouldn't call the worship center the "sanctuary" because to say "sanctuary" seemed to make it some kind of a ritualistic, special place. Yet when we say to our children, "Don't run in the sanctuary" or "Don't make noise in the sanctuary," these admonitions reveal that we do consider it to be a place set apart. Certainly, it *is* a special place for us because it is one of the few places where we gather together for

---

10 William Barclay, *The Ten Commandments for Today,* Harper and Row, 1973.

the corporate worship of God, but it is not an object of worship. We must keep in mind that an idol is anything that usurps the place God should have.

In the same way, we must beware of worshipping the ritual of worship; although the music is exquisite, the sermon brilliant and the hour exciting! Even the ritual of the Lord's Supper can become the object of worship. However, we must never substitute the ordinance for the reality of the Lord's death. True worship is being in the presence of Almighty God and experiencing an encounter with Him so that He is lifted up—not the preacher, not the acts of worship, but the Lord Himself, who makes demands on our response to Him.

It was ironic to me when I visited Moscow in the mid-1990's that the Kremlin, populated from 1917 by a regime that passionately embraced atheism, included many old buildings which recalled the faith of an earlier day. There are churches honoring the Archangel Michael, the Twelve Apostles, the Annunciation, and the Deposition of the Virgin's Robe. There are Wall Towers dedicated to Saint Peter, Saint Nicholas and the Savior.

There is also the Cathedral of the Dormition of the Virgin, an imposing place where in the past the royalty and the military would come before battles, asking God's blessings and, after battles, celebrating the victory God had given to them. In this cathedral, in the midst of all the beautiful trappings of ancient orthodoxy is the "pew" of the first tsar, Ivan IV, often called Ivan the Terrible. I could picture him bowed and worshipping in the little cathedral-like structure within which he sat. Yet, I remember with shock, he would leave that place of worship to commit some of the most atrocious and cruel acts ever imagined. He killed his own son, Ivan. He married seven times, ridding himself of his unwanted wives by forcing them to become nuns. His reverence for the place and his homage to the artifacts it contained had absolutely nothing to do with his behavior or lifestyle. He had substituted the ritual of worship for God, as surely as if it were a graven image.

If we go into the sanctuary and participate in worship and if we leave there with our behavior unaffected, then we have not worshipped. We are little different from Ivan the Terrible. Worship and service are inseparable. The God that we worship is the God that we serve.

After God's command in Exodus that we should bow down and serve no other gods, He explains, "*...for I, the Lord your God, am a jealous God...*" The adjective "jealous" may seem strange when used in expressing God's response to us, but how better could the intensity of His love for us be expressed? His next phrase, "*...visiting the iniquity of the fathers on the children, on the third and the fourth generations of those who hate Me*" is not a threat to punish our children and grandchildren but a warning that our actions carry over into succeeding generations. The greatest legacy we can give our offspring is to help them to love God and obey Him. God affirmed the principle when He ended this commandment with a promise, "*...showing* *lovingkindness to thousands, to those who love Me and keep My commandments."*

I honestly believe the members of my family are receiving blessings because my parents were faithful to the Lord and my parents reaped the blessings of the Lord because both of their parents knew the Lord. I became a believer as a boy, not because I had an inquisitive religious mind but because I was being reared in an environment where Christ was an intimate part. It was very natural for me to trust the Lord because of the example of my parents' trust in the Lord and their parents' trust and their grandparents' trust.

A woman told of an incident which helped her know she had really come of age. In her family there was a lovely golden vase, a very special family treasure, which had been in the family for years and years. It was placed very prominently on the mantel in the living room of their home. One day when she was still an inquisitive little girl she reached up to the vase, wanting to examine it more closely. But when she touched the vase it tipped over, fell off the mantel and crashed onto the floor, broken into many, many pieces. The child burst into tears and her mother, hearing the noise, rushed into the room. When the woman told the story years later, she said her mother's first response was a look of relief. She said, "My mother picked me up and pulled me to her and said, 'Oh, I'm so grateful!' When I heard you crying, I thought you had been hurt!"

She had broken the family treasure but her mother was not concerned about it. She was concerned about her little daughter who had broken it. "At that moment," she said, "I realized that I was the family treasure."[11]

We are God's treasures, and He wants us for Himself. He is indeed a "jealous" God.

If we find it hard to assume the relationship God wants with us, only because we feel the need for an image to see, a form to flesh out, all we have to do is look to Jesus. The New Testament tells us the clearest image of God is Jesus Christ. When Philip, the apostle who had traveled with Jesus for more than three years, said to Jesus just before the crucifixion, *"Lord, show us the Father, and it is enough for us."* Jesus said, *"...He who has seen Me has seen the Father..."* (John 14:8, 9).

Later, Paul would describe Jesus to the Colossians: *"He is the image of the invisible God..."* (Colossians 1:15). To the Corinthians he would speak of the glory of Christ, *"...who is the image of God"* (2 Corinthians 4:4). In Hebrews we read that *"(Jesus) is the radiance of His glory and the exact representation of His nature, and upholds all things by the word of His power"* (Hebrews 1:3).

Jesus' words at the time of the temptation by the devil reveal His own recognition of His Godlikeness. To the devil He said, *"You shall not put the Lord your God to the*

---

11 Frank W. Harrington, "The Vital Signs of a Vital Church," *Great Preaching 1992*, edited by Michael Duduit, The Preaching Library, page 9.

test" (Matthew 4:7). Then, when Satan offered Jesus all the kingdoms of the world if only He would worship him, Jesus gave the strongest possible endorsement of the second commandment. He said, *"Go, Satan! For it is written, 'You shall worship the Lord your God, and serve Him only'"* (Matthew 4:10).

The scripture continues by saying the devil then left Jesus, and the angels came and ministered to Him. If we denounce our idols and refuse to bow down to other than our true God, we may not have angels coming to minister to us, but we will have something far better: the lovingkindness of God Himself! This is the promise He gives us in the second commandment.

Reverence for God's Name

You shall not take the name of the Lord your God in vain, for the Lord will not leave him unpunished who takes His name in vain.

Exodus 20:7

In the years following the Civil War, Robert E. Lee, the defeated general, was respected not only by the armies he had led but by people across the nation. After the defeat of the Confederate armies, penniless and without a job, he was approached by a group of investors from the North who said, "We're planning to start an insurance company and we want to use your name. As honorary president of the company, you will have no duties or responsibilities and will be paid a very comfortable salary." Firmly, definitely, Robert E. Lee answered, "I've lost everything because of my service to the Confederacy. All I have left is my name, and it isn't for sale."[12]

---

12 John Bisagno, *Positive Obedience*, Zondervan, 1979, pages 25-26.

I remember, when I was a boy how my father and my grandfather talked to me about the importance of our name. They wanted their children to know about our family name and our ancestry. They helped us to see that inappropriate behavior could be injurious and even slanderous to our family name.

Throughout recorded time having a good name has been important. Often the character of a person was expressed in a name. In biblical days names were so significant that they were sometimes changed to reflect new aspects of their characters as events transformed them.

Before the birth of Isaac God said, *"No longer shall your name be called Abram, but your name shall be Abraham; for I have made you the father of a multitude of nations"* (Genesis 17:5). God gave Abraham a son, Isaac, and through Isaac would come descendants who would be numberless as the sands of the seashore.

When Jacob deceived his twin brother Esau, he seemed to be well suited to his name, which means *deceiver*. But after he wrestled with an angel, his life took on a new significance, and God changed his name from Jacob to Israel, meaning *prince of God*. Jacob became the father of the sons of Israel, head of the tribes out of which the Messiah would come.

In the New Testament (Acts 4:36-37) there is a story about a Levite named Joseph, a native of Cypress. He was such an encourager that the Apostles changed his name to Barnabas, which means *son of encouragement*. His new name reflected his character. There was also Simon, who came to be called Petros or Peter. The name meant *the rock*. "*Upon this rock*," Jesus said, "*I will build my church; and the gates of Hades will not overpower it*" (Matthew 16:18).

Parents search diligently to select the best names for their children. When my wife Sheila was pregnant with our first child, we bought books with suggested names. We determined to use her maiden name, "King," if it was a boy. We also desired to use a name from the Bible that would help shape his character. I suggested "James." Then his whole name would be King James. We could call him Art, a shortened form of Arthur for the Authorized Version of the Bible.

Fortunately we chose another name, Jeremy King Everett. Jeremy comes from the biblical name "Jeremiah," which means prophet to the nations. However, during those first sleepless months we were reminded that Jeremiah was also the weeping prophet. We carefully selected the name "Rachel" for our second child. She is, thanks to the grace of God and maternal genes, pretty like the biblical Rachel, who was the beautiful wife of Jacob. I pray that the Lord will one day give her a godly child like the biblical Rachel's son Joseph.

Understanding the significance of a name enhances our understanding of the third commandment. The importance of a name is reflected in the fact that, most of the time, a person's name is the first thing we know about him or her and begins the process of getting to know that person.

Knowing a person's name gives us access to that person. Knowing God's name, in the intimate sense of the word, helps us to realize God's accessibility to us. When Moses asked God His name (Exodus 3), God began the infinitely important process of self-disclosure: "My name is 'I am.' My name is 'I will continuously be who I have always been.'" This form of God's name was brought over into English as *Yahweh*. The story is told that when the ancient scribes were transcribing the scripture, they were so sensitive to the sacredness of God's name that when they came to the Tetragramaton, the four letters (*yod, he, vav, he*) used to represent this name of God, they would fast and pray before they would even write the representation. They bathed themselves and put on new garments. They took new quills. Only then would they write **YHWH**! Afterwards they bathed themselves again, burned the quill, burned their clothes, and prayed and fasted before continuing to write out the scripture.

God's name was so sacred and holy that the ancient Hebrews would not speak it. Eventually they began to use the word *Adonai*, which means *Master* or *Lord*. After many years the vowels from *Adonai* and the consonants from *Yahweh* were made into a hybrid word, *Jehovah*, which could be said in the place of *YHWH*.

Other names we find for God enhance our understanding of who He is. In Isaiah 7:14 is found the familiar *Immanuel*, meaning God with us. In Isaiah 9:6 we are given *Wonderful Counselor, Mighty God, Eternal Father, Prince of Peace*. All of these names are descriptive of God's character and therefore increase our access to Him. God has revealed Himself to us by telling us His name. It is a sad and remarkable—even ironic—fact that the ancient Hebrews would not even pronounce a name that in our society is so lightly trivialized.

In this third commandment we are admonished about the reverence for God's holy name: *"You shall not take the name of the Lord your God in vain."* This concept is difficult to understand. What does it mean to take God's name in *vain*? The word translated vain can also be translated emptiness or nothingness. It is commonplace today for individuals to have vocabularies which are characterized by irreverence and frequent use of God's name as an expletive. In our time we not only use the word God (*Yahweh* in Hebrew, *Deus* in Latin, *Bog* in Russian, *Gott* in the Teutonic languages, *Theos* in Greek) in this empty fashion, but we do the same with the name of our Lord, our divine Savior, Jesus. Consider that the misuse of the name Jesus is a profaning of the One who chose to take our sins upon Himself. This profanity has become so ordinary and commonplace that we hardly notice it!

One translation of the Bible interprets the third commandment: *"You shall not make wrongful use of the name of the Lord your God."* In some places the word *lie* is used, meaning *falsehood*. God surely expects when we use His name to bind a promise, such a pledge is sacred and not to be broken.

Three such uses come readily to mind. The oaths taken in courts of law and in inaugurations of office and ending "so help me God" are so commonly broken as to be laughable. Jesus Himself taught that oaths should be unnecessary. The simple word of a person should be that person's bond (Matthew 5:33-37). The marriage vows taken "in the name of the Father, the Son and the Holy Spirit" are sometimes spoken with the knowledge that when difficulty arises the vows can be forgotten. Also, when we have taken God's name *Christian* upon ourselves at the time of conversion and yet live un-Christian lives, we have made wrongful use of His name, have actually lied against it.

God's name is also trivialized by commercialization. I hear of "Christian" entertainers who charge extravagant amounts for one evening's entertainment in the name of Christ. It is almost as if they are saying, "Pastor, if your church will pay me a certain amount of money, then I'll come and tell them Jesus loves them and has died for their sins." I have a publisher friend who refuses to attend the giant Christian trade shows because there are so many companies displaying shoddy merchandise which make a buck from commercialization of sublime Christian concepts.

Most of the pastors and church staff members that I know make far less than they would earn in other professions. Yet regardless of our salaries are we willing to pick up at any moment and follow Christ wherever He leads regardless of income?

It is also tempting to use God's name to manipulate other people. Preachers may stand before a congregation and say, "God told me to say this," or "God told you to do that." We are tempted to use the name of God to accomplish our own agendas. When we speak for God, we had better be sure that it is God Who has spoken to us. The only way I know for certain that we can speak for God is to speak His words in the context in which they are written.

God has spoken to us in the third commandment. He promises that the *"Lord will not leave him unpunished who takes His name in vain."* When we treat God as unholy, God will hold us accountable. There are several instances in the Bible of persons who were punished for their failure to properly regard God's holiness. One is an interesting story in Leviticus 10:1-2.

> *"Now Nadab and Abihu, the sons of Aaron, took their respective firepans, and after putting fire in them, placed incense on it and offered strange fire before the Lord, which He had not commanded them. And fire came out from the presence of the Lord and consumed them, and they died before the Lord."*

These two did not present their offering in the manner God had prescribed, and they were punished for their neglect.

Another example is Moses. There was no more humble and righteous man on the earth, but he was still very human. When Moses trivialized God's instruction to him, the Lord had occasion to say to Moses and Aaron, *"Because you have not believed Me, to treat Me as holy in the sight of the sons of Israel, therefore you shall not bring this assembly into the land which I have given them"* (Numbers 20:12). How Moses heart must have ached when he learned he would miss actually entering the land of promise. What a disappointment this punishment must have been!

In Acts 5:3 we read that Ananias and his wife Sapphira attempted to convince the church they loved God in a sacrificial way. However, they lied about giving the Lord the full price of some land they had sold. As a consequence, God struck them dead. They took the name of the Lord in vain and received His punishment.

There are other consequences as well. When men like David Koresh (the leader of the Branch Davidian sect near Waco, Texas), claim to be Christ or representatives of Christ, then commit acts of violence in the name of God, the hearts of unbelievers are hardened and the task of believers becomes immensely more difficult. Historically, when the church itself has tried to use manipulative power or political muscle unbelievers have been made more resistant to Christ. Abuse of God's name can result in consequences we would have never dreamed, yet if our actions are what God desires, the result may be beyond our wildest dreams.

What does God desire? In Jeremiah 33:3 the Lord says, *"Call to Me and I will answer you, and I will tell you great and mighty things, which you do not know."* God wants us to call on His name! The writer of the Psalms knows this. He sings *"O Lord, our Lord, How majestic is Thy name in all the earth..."* (Psalm 8:1) and *"Ascribe to the Lord the glory due to His name..."* (Psalm 29:2). Psalm 34:3 exhorts *"O magnify the Lord with me, and let us exalt His name together."*

The New Testament tells us in numerous places why we should do these things. Paul wrote,*"Whoever will call upon the name of the Lord will be saved"* (Romans 10:13). Jesus said to His disciples (and to us): *"Until now you have asked for nothing in My name; ask and you will receive, so that your joy may be made full"* (John 16:24).

To use God's name in any other way is to treat His name lightly, to underestimate His power, to scorn his very presence. God's demand in the third commandment that we not misuse His name is consistent with His gracious covenant and steadfastness. To call upon Him is to call upon His presence and power.

Let us exalt the name of the Lord our God!

Celebrating the Lord's Day

"Remember the sabbath day, to keep it holy. Six days you shall labor and do all your work, but the seventh day is a sabbath of the Lord your God; in it you shall not do any work, you or your son or your daughter, your male or your female servant or your cattle or your sojourner who stays with you. For in six days the Lord made the heavens and the earth, the sea and all that is in them, and rested on the seventh day; therefore the Lord blessed the sabbath day and made it holy.

Exodus 20:8-11

In his book *In the Eye of the Storm* Max Lucado tells the story about Chippy, the little parakeet whose owner stuck the vacuum cleaner hose in the bottom of his cage to suck up all the loose bird seed. When she turned away to answer the phone, the predicable happened. She heard a desperate "cheep" and Chippy was gone. Dropping the phone, she removed the dust bag. There was Chippy, alive, bedraggled, dazed, and dirty. A bath in the sink reduced the poor bird to a mass of shivering feathers. A blast of hot air from the hair dryer compounded the shock.

In answer to a question a few weeks later, the owner said, "Chippy is alive and healthy. He just doesn't sing much anymore."[13]

Often we feel like Chippy, as if we have been sucked in, washed up, and blown over. We don't feel like singing either. God knows this about us and knows the need we have for a respite from daily life. God knew the same about the ancient Israelites.

Long before God spoke to Moses on Mount Sinai, the Israelites had been nomadic shepherds, roaming the arid land and struggling to survive. Later, as slaves in Egypt, they lost many of their traditions. They may have come to Sinai feeling like Chippy, sucked in, washed up, and blown over. The Lord at Sinai gave them the fourth commandment, which deals with rest and reverence. This admonition was actually God's response to Israel's need.

In this, the longest of all the commandments (and one of only two that are not negatively expressed), the people were instructed to set aside a day of rest after six days of work.

Some people translate the word *Sabbath* to mean *seventh*, but it is from the Hebrew word that means *rest* or *cessation of labor*. The Sabbath did not originate on Mount Sinai.

---

13 Max Lucado, *In the Eye of the Storm*, Word, 1991, page 11.

It was part of the very creation of life: after the days of working/creating God rested on the seventh day. When He created us He built into us a working/resting clock. Just as the moon causes the tide to come in and go out, there seems to be within every person a need to work and a need to rest. God's command to us to rest is more than an attempt on His part to make us feel better physically. It is an act with cosmic implications because God's resting is a divine act that builds into the created order of things a working/resting rhythm.

On Sinai, He set forth the commandments and said, *"Remember the Sabbath day to keep it holy,"* as though it were something they were already experiencing. Even before this commandment was given, while the Israelites were in the Wilderness of Sin on the way from the Red Sea to Mount Sinai (Exodus 16:1), God showed the day of rest to be a basic life principle for His people.

During the Exodus from Egypt, the Israelites ran out of food and God responded to their need: *"Behold, I will rain bread from heaven for you."* Every day, God said, they should pick up just enough manna for that day's food because more would *"breed worms and become foul."* But, He said, on the sixth day they should gather enough manna for that day and for the seventh because the seventh was the day of rest. On the sixth day those who were greedy and gathered more than they needed for the seventh day saw their manna spoil but those who didn't gather enough had plenty! God was teaching them the principle of resting and labor.

Eventually, after centuries of interaction with other nations, the Jewish principle of keeping the Sabbath gave way to Pharasaism, which contained numerous regulations and laws concerning activities prohibited on that day. Thirty-nine different categories of work prohibited on the Sabbath day were developed into some incredibly detailed and difficult-to-follow rules. In their apparently sincere attempts to responsibly interpret the Law of God, the Pharisees missed entirely the point of the Law. They began to insist on rules and regulations to cover every conceivable event that might happen to a man. There came a passion for definition and for the fragmentation of principles into rules and regulations.

For instance, it was against the law of the Sabbath to carry a burden on the Sabbath day. Is a child a burden? No, the ruling said the child is not a burden unless he has a stone in his hand because a stone is a burden. A person could *pull* a stick on the Sabbath day but not *push* it. All of these restrictions were gradually producing a nation of people who were so intent on tithing tiny spices that they *"neglected the weightier matters of the law."*

Some Christian groups still retain remnants of this compulsive legalistic observance. The time is not too far past when on Sundays there was a cessation of all kinds of activities for Christians. On that day we were very careful about where we would go and what we would do.

I remember as a boy that our family would not go to a restaurant for Sunday lunch because eating out would cause someone else to work. Recreation in the afternoon after church was not an option for some. A friend told me that one summer when he was a college student he attended a Bible conference at a campground in Cantonment, Florida. On Sunday afternoon when there were no planned meetings he took a checker board and checkers from cabin to cabin trying, without success, to find someone to play checkers with him. Finally, the elderly camp director cornered him and said, "We don't play checkers on Sunday around here."

Today we are not likely to be guilty of being legalistic on the Lord's Day for we have gone to the other extreme. Many do not work on Sunday but certainly play on Sunday. Sunday is often a day for recreation or work around the house or ball games for children.

Joy Davidman writes of an imaginary extraterrestrial visitor who was sent to earth to report on the religious life of humans. Knowing that Sunday was supposed to be a holy day, he deduced immediately that the day was aptly named, for a wide variety of rituals were performed in homage to the Sun god. Some people anointed themselves with oil and prostrated themselves before the sun. Others gathered in huge open stadiums where two sets of strangely vested priests performed strenuous adulations before the cheering crowd. If the visitor's report were to be graded on logic, it no doubt received a galactic A![14]

---

14 Joy Davidman, pages 49-50.

If the fourth commandment is to be interpreted literally, then we are grossly violating it. If on the other hand, we ignore it completely, we are missing a great opportunity to affirm the covenant God. I personally believe that God's requirement for our use of the day falls somewhere between the two extremes. Obviously we no longer live in a primitive society, and certain services must be provided (by working persons!) to keep the infrastructure of our complicated society viable. On the other hand, we must take seriously the covenant nature God intended this commandment to convey.

Worship is as important to the observance as is rest. As we worship we are reminded of the Cross, the empty tomb, the resurrection, the completed work of Christ. We worship, we praise, and we are restored.

Some Christian groups have kept to the custom of observing the seventh day of the week, the ancient Sabbath. Why, they challenge, do other Christians observe the first day of the week? They contend that such observance is not biblical.

While the early Christians were still Jews and would have continued to observe the seventh day Sabbath, the first day of the week became an important holy day, for on that day the most significant event of their lives had occurred—the Resurrection. Also, it was on the first day of the week when the disciples were gathered together that the Holy Spirit came. They were filled with the Spirit of God, and the church was birthed by the touch of God's hand. It is no wonder that the church began to assemble together on the first day of the week.

In the New Testament, the Lord's Day, the first day of the week, represented Christ, who was the substance of what was promised. *"Therefore let no one act as your judge in regard to food or drink or in respect to a festival or a new moon or a Sabbath day—things which are a mere shadow of what is to come; but the substance belongs to Christ"* (Colossians 2:16-17). The Sabbath of the Old Testament foreshadowed what was to come.

In Acts 20:7 we learn that on the first day of the week the congregation at Troas met to break bread. In Corinthians Paul told the congregation to put aside on the first day of the week a collection for the Jerusalem church (1 Corinthians 16:2). John uses the expression "The Lord's Day" in Revelation 1:10. These references exemplify the change. Beginning in the second century we can find literary evidence that the Lord's Day had supplanted the Sabbath for Christians, whether they were Jewish or not.

I doubt that Jesus himself would have been concerned about making a switch from one day to another. He dealt with the substance, or the real meaning and purpose of the commandment. As a result, Jesus was in constant trouble with the authorities, whose concern was not with the substance but with following correctly the thirty-nine categories and the fifteen hundred rules and interpretations.

Sabbath violation was used more than any of the other commandments as an excuse to accuse Jesus of heresy. The second chapter of Mark records that on a Sabbath day Jesus and His disciples were walking among the grain fields. The disciples began to break off the heads of the stalks of grain, rub out the grain and eat. Apparently, some of the folks who were walking with the group were there, not to get to know Him and learn from Him but to find things that were wrong with His faith and to trap Him. When they saw what the disciples were doing, they knew they had Him! The disciples were accused of reaping and threshing on the Sabbath, which was strictly forbidden by law.

The scribes and Pharisees said to Him, "Are you going to let your followers violate the fourth commandment by not keeping the Sabbath day holy?"

> *"And He said to them, 'Have you never read what David did when he was in need and he and his companions became hungry; how he entered the house of God in the time of Abiathar the high priest, and ate the consecrated bread, which is not lawful for anyone to eat except the priests, and he also gave it to those who were with him?' Jesus said to them, 'The Sabbath was made for man, and not man for the Sabbath. So the Son of Man is Lord even of the Sabbath'"* (Mark 2:25-28).

In the very next chapter (Mark 3:1-5) Jesus riles them again.

> *"He entered again into a synagogue; and a man was there whose hand was withered. They were watching Him to*

see if He would heal him on the Sabbath, so that they might accuse Him. He said to the man with the withered hand, 'Get up and come forward!' And He said to them, 'Is it lawful to do good or to do harm on the Sabbath, to save a life or to kill?' But they kept silent. After looking around at them with anger, grieved at their hardness of heart, He said to the man, 'Stretch out your hand.' And he stretched it out, and his hand was restored."

His defense, as set forth in the Sermon on the Mount (Matthew 5:17-19), was hard for them to understand. Jesus said, *"Do not think that I came to abolish the Law or the Prophets; I did not come to abolish, but to fulfill."* But this idea was very difficult for the religious leaders to understand, especially since He was disregarding their fifteen hundred rules.

What does the Sabbath day mean to us today? It is impossible for us to live life at the meaningful level where God wants us without a time of rest and worship. It is true that we worship the Lord every day with Bible study, prayer and a quiet time. Yet for many this lasts only fifteen to thirty minutes a day. We need the full Lord's Day for restorative purposes.

Can a picnic with the family on Sunday honor His name? Indeed it can. Do family meals, friends, fellowship and worship fulfill God's command? Indeed they do. As John Bisagno, the former pastor of First Baptist Church of Houston wrote, every decision should be made in light of a holy consideration of the questions: "Is God glorified?

Is God pleased? Would I be happy for Christ to be with me in this activity? Would He do it? Can I honor Him as I do it?"[15]

There is a difference between our day of rest and that of the Israelites. They spent the seventh day looking back on what God did? We spend the first day of the week looking forward to what God is doing. It is on the Lord's Day, the first day of the week, that we can—no, that we must—shut out business, personal goals and animosities as we focus on the Lord and let our spirits be energized and our souls restored.

---

15 John Bisagno, Positive Obedience, Zondervan, 1979, page 32.

Worthy of Respect

Honor your father and your mother, that your days may be prolonged in the land which the Lord your God gives you.

Exodus 20:12

Joy Davidman wrote about a man had lived a rich and full life. This is a part of his story.

When he was advanced in years and had come to the time in his life that we may all come to eventually, he was living with his son, his daughter-in-law and their children because he could no longer care for himself. His hands trembled most of the time, and eating was particularly embarrassing because his food would shake off his fork or spoon. At the table he sometimes made a clattering sound with his eating utensils against the surface of the table. When he tried to feed himself, he would miss his mouth about as often as he would find it. Sometimes he would drool or drip food on the table.

Finally the daughter-in-law couldn't take it any longer, and so she and her husband banished this old man, his father, to the corner at mealtime. They put him on a stool to eat from an earthenware bowl out of sight of the children. Many times he would look wistfully toward the table. One day his hands trembled more than usual so that he knocked over the bowl, which shattered on the floor, scattering food. The daughter-in-law stood over him threateningly and said, "That does it. If you're going to act like a pig, we'll feed you like one." They made a little trough and he was forced to eat from that.

After a few days the old man's son noticed his own four-year-old son playing with pieces of wood. When he asked the child what he was doing, the youngster responded, as he looked up at his dad for approval, "I'm making a trough for you and Mother so that when you get old I can feed you."

The mother and father looked at each other for several moments in silence, and both began to weep. Then they very gently brought the old father back to the table. They gave him a comfortable place to sit and fed him from a plate. Never again did they scold him when he clattered or spilled things.[16]

This old story could have happened last week. Besides the cases we have heard of in which elderly parents are blatantly abused, most of us can list examples we personally know who suffer from neglect. Ours is one

---

16 Joy Davidman, page 60-61.

of the few societies that does not have a unique built-in respect for the elderly, a recognition of their value. It is a very strange thing that we would not love and respect those who gave us life itself, who nurtured us as children, and who sacrificed many of the pleasures of life so that we might have a better life than they did. It's an amazing culture that would not value or would turn its back on those who have served so ably and so well.

Honor your father and your mother, that your days may be prolonged in the land which the Lord your God gives you.

As we consider this commandment, we are reminded that it shows us that God's plan for human living is based on the family being the basic unit of all the human relationships. Genesis 1-3 shows us that when God made Adam and Eve He created the home before there was ever a temple or a synagogue or a church. There was a family unit before there was any organized religious activity or civil government. It was the family that was the very foundation of all human relationships.

When the family erodes and ultimately dissolves in a society, society will erode and dissolve. It is impossible to maintain a viable society without the family. We cannot ignore the problems and difficulties facing the home and expect that society will remain intact. Our world is built on very fragile relationships.

Very soon eighty percent of the population of the world will be living in cities. In Africa, South America, Asia, Europe, and Japan, as well as North America, people will be jammed into huge mega-cities of ten to twenty million persons. When people are jammed together, tension and anxiety, disease and hunger increase out of proportion to the population increase. The larger the cities become, the more imperative it is that families be strong and healthy.

There are strong forces in contemporary culture which would change the way that parents and children relate to each other. Rolf Zettersten, in his book *Train Up a Child*, discusses the so-called Children's Rights Movement. "The first major triumph for the movement," he says, "occurred in Sweden in 1979 when it became illegal for parents to spank their children. An emergency twenty-four-hour phone line was established by the Swedish parliament so kids could report their parents' violations of this law. A few years later, the Swedish government amended its Constitution to grant children the right to 'divorce' their parents."[17]

It is imperative that we have men who are husbands first of all and women who are wives first of all who become parents who understand they are not their children's buddies but their parents. Sad to say, many times it is the parents who train their children to dishonor them. Several years ago, according to William Barclay, there was a pamphlet distributed by the Houston police department headed *How to Train Your Child to Be a Delinquent*.[18] These twelve suggestions are still appropriate for both parents and children.

---

17 Rolf Zettersten, *Train up a Child*, Living Books, 1994.
18 Barclay, pages 57-58.

1. GIVE YOUR CHILD EVERYTHING HE/SHE WANTS. Begin at infancy to give the child everything he wants. In this way, he will grow up to believe the world owes him a living. After all, we know how it was when we were children and we were deprived of some of those basic things in life, like new cleats for our baseball shoes or the latest cosmetic. We want our children to have everything that other kids have so they won't feel psychologically deprived.

2. WHEN YOUR CHILD USES BAD LANGUAGE LAUGH AT HIM. LET HIM KNOW THAT YOU THINK IT'S CUTE. When a child comes out with some special four-letter word, we wonder where he got it. The kid couldn't have gotten it from home. Then we realize that he's been with the in-laws. We can't wait to tell our friends how funny it is.

3. DO NOT GIVE YOUR CHILD ANY SPIRITUAL TRAINING. Why not wait until they become adults? Then they can decide for themselves what, if any, religious decisions they want to make. This method is as effective as waiting until they get a desire to learn before enrolling them in school.

4. AVIOD USE OF THE WORD *WRONG*. A guilt complex may result, which will condition him to believe later, when he is arrested for stealing a car, that society is against him and he is being persecuted.

5. PICK UP AFTER YOUR CHILDREN WHEN THEY ARE SMALL. And when they're older, continue to

pick up after them: their shoes, their books—whatever is lying around, especially in their rooms. That way they can learn that everyone else is responsible for their behavior.

6. LET YOUR CHILDREN READ WHATEVER THEY WANT TO READ (or watch whatever they want too watch). Be sure to sterilize their drinking glasses because we don't want them to get germs, but let their minds feast on garbage. Let them read any magazine or book or see anything on television or go to any movie they want to.

7. QUARREL FREQUENTLY WITH YOUR SPOUSE IN THE PRESENCE OF YOUR CHILDREN. They will become more and more insecure in a very volatile world. In this way they will not be too shocked when the home is broken up later.

8. IT IS ESSENTIAL TO GIVE YOUR CHILDREN PLENTY OF SPENDING MONEY. They need enough money so that they won't feel a sense of frustration. Why should they have things as tough as you did? Don't let them go to work.

9. MAKE ABSOLUTELY CERTAIN THAT CHILDREN'S SENSUAL DESIRES ARE FULFILLED. You should supply promptly without question whatever it is that they want to eat or whatever they want to drink. Take them wherever they want to go. Denial may lead to harmful frustration.

10. TAKE YOUR CHILD'S SIDE IN EVERY ISSUE. Take his part against neighbors, teachers, and policemen so that the child understands that they are prejudiced against him.

11. WHEN HE/SHE GETS INTO TROUBLE, BE READY WITH THE EXCUSE, "I'VE NEVER BEEN ABLE TO DO ANYTHING WITH THIS CHILD." How can parents be blamed for a child's behavior when they have tried to give the child everything?

12. BE PREPARED FOR A LIFE OF GRIEF. It's certain to come!

At the church where I was pastor we honored our graduating high school seniors with a breakfast at a country club. The following Sunday the seniors wore their caps and gowns and were a part of the processional in the Sunday morning service so that we could celebrate together this tremendous achievement in their lives.

Sometimes we have the dedication of babies and the graduation breakfast for the seniors on the same morning. Life passes so quickly that I almost feel the mortar-boarded seniors are the same babies we dedicated the week before! Life is so brief that parents can't waste time on the superficial and miss the urgent responsibility of being mothers and fathers to our sons and our daughters. In the same way, children hardly have enough time in their fast-paced, activity-filled lives to properly honor their parents.

Some of us have gotten an "A" in "Honoring," but for the rest of us there are some "A's" of a different kind that may help us.

ALLEGIANCE

If we don't teach our children to obey their parents, then they will be ill-equipped to obey any of the other authorities in life. In Ephesians 6:1, Paul invokes the ancient commandment and admonishes the children of Ephesus to *"obey your parents."* The word obey in the Greek comes from the word meaning to hear. The first step in obedience is to hear, to listen. Among many families this is a dying, or perhaps already lost, art. We must listen to each other in the family. Children must practice allegiance to their parents by obeying them.

God has given parents as authorities to give life and strength and direction to help mold children in life. Unfortunately we live in a society where some parents abuse their children. Unbelievable as it is that a father or mother would sexually or physically or emotionally abuse a child when that stewardship responsibility has been given by God, nevertheless it happens. There is a strong qualification in Ephesians 6. *"Children obey your parents in the Lord."* Children have no responsibility to obey a parent in something that is specifically contrary to God's Word.

ADMIRATION

From the word *honor* comes the idea of admiration. This word translated *honor* in the English from the Hebrew meant *heavy* or, more specifically, *fat*. In a society where few had sufficient food, persons who were fat gave evidence that they had plenty and so must have been wealthy or certainly successful in their responsibility and therefore due respect. Kids won't gain points by calling their parents "fat," but they must honor them by showing them admiration due respected personages.

APPRECIATION

If a person asks, "Why should I show appreciation to my parents?" I am quick to respond, "Because you're alive." If my mother did absolutely nothing more for me than to give me life, then she has sacrificed greatly for me.

When my wife Sheila and I were going through our first pregnancy, we both had morning sickness and both gained weight! When we were getting ready for the second one, she said, "If we go to Lamaze classes, they'll let you go into the delivery room." I said, "The last place in the world I ever want to be is in the delivery room. Let them knock you out and knock me out. Then when the baby is born and can say 'Yes sir,' bring us back!"

The discomfort, inconvenience, and pain that a mother goes through in those nine months of pregnancy and in giving birth are real sacrifices for her child. Furthermore, in those first weeks and months of life outside of the womb a baby is a heavy burden who robs her of rest and adds unimaginable stress and anxiety to her life.

We owe our mothers a debt of appreciation if only because they gave us life, but many of us are blessed with mothers who gave much more than that. Many of us have or had the kind of mothers who would have laid down their lives for us—and still would! Our appreciation for such selflessness may only be realized after we become parents ourselves.

AGREEMENT

To honor means to be in agreement with parents. This is not to say that there should not be the inevitable testing as adolescents learn to be independent; or that differing attitudes should not be thoroughly discussed with an eye to resolution. Agreement in this sense means that children must make a real effort to understand where their parents are coming from and must put major effort into living with them in an atmospher of courtesy and understanding. Incidentally, parents have responsibility in this area, too. Agreement means difficult work on both sides, each trying to see the other's point of view. Love is an act of will, and love is a special kind of work.

ATTENTION

Giving attention to parents is not just a matter of listening to them when we are children but of taking care of them when they are older. It is a curious thing that two parents can take care of two to five children who need everything from diapers to orthodontists and later those same two to five children can't take care of those same parents when they are elderly. We have an unusual phenomenon in our nation. Many older people, even some who are retired, are taking care of more elderly parents. Some of these "children" are grandparents themselves. Because of the unusual longevity of people in our society we have more and more challenges in the care of aging parents.

Jesus gave us a beautiful example. When he was suffering that excruciating death on the cross, he still gave attention to his mother. He turned to John, standing by his mother, and said, "Here is your mother. Take care of her."

AGAPE

The final "A" of these clues designed to help us obey the fifth commandment can be termed *Agape*. The Apostle Paul's description of this love in First Corinthians 13 is a model for the love we should show our parents. *"This love of which I speak is slow to lose patience—it looks for a way of being constructive. It is not possessive; it is neither anxious to impress nor does it cherish inflated ideas of its own importance."* The Phillips translation continues, *"Love has good manners and does not pursue selfish advantage. It is not touchy. It does not keep account of evil or gloat over the wickedness of other people. On the contrary it is glad with all good men when truth prevails. Love knows no limit to its endurance, no end to its trust, no fading of its hope; it can outlast anything. It is, in fact, the one thing that still stands when everything else has fallen."*

It seems to me that all of the other "A's" are summed up in Agape Love. The universal application of this scripture would work miracles on all familial relationships. How many of us are estranged from parents or children, brothers or sister, or others from the family circle? In Dr. Paul Meier's introduction to David Stoops' book *Forgiving our Parents Forgiving Ourselves* there is a word of advice.

Deep down inside each of us is a longing for a satisfying and lasting family relationship. The task for each of us is to somehow come to grips with our family and to resolve the basic issues we have with the individuals within our family. The only way I know to resolve the issues of the past in our families is through forgiveness. The alternative is to hold onto grudges, and we pay a tremendous price for doing this…Taking the effort to analyze and understand the dynamics of our families of origin will help us to take control of our lives, and to move in new and healthier directions. Unless forgiveness is part of the equation, our analysis and understanding will leave us still caught in the family dysfunction.[19]

The fifth commandment comes immediately after the four that pertain to our relationship with God. Think of the significance of this placement! Its significance may be seen in the reiteration of the honor commandment in Leviticus 20:9, which makes the penalty for dishonoring parents the same as the penalty for dishonoring God noted in Exodus 21:17—death! Consider also that in the commandments' order this one is listed first in the group which deals with our relationships with other persons.

In this fifth commandment God gives us instruction, then offers us a pledge. God promises that the faithful, who

---

19 David Stoop, *Forgiving our Parents Forgiving Ourselves*, Regal, 2011.

honor and obey their parents, will enjoy abundant life and will live long on the earth. Obviously, extended years of life might result from our attention to our parents' wise and caring requirements for our health and well-being. Also, by heeding our parents' advice we would avoid some of the mistakes that they or their parents have made or observed as they've lived their lives and we might thereby extend our days. God's promise, however, refers to more than long-living. He is reiterating His covenant with Israel, the same covenant that bore its ultimate fruit in the coming of Jesus. If our relationship with Jesus is the primary one in our lives, then the difficulties inherent in all the ramifications of this honor commandment can be overcome.

The Sanctity of Life

You shall not murder.

Exodus 20:13

Joan was in the sixth week of her first semester in college when she found out that she was pregnant. After she had graduated from high school, she spent two years on her own. During that time, estranged from her church and her parents, she had experimented with a lifestyle that was foreign to her. She became involved with a married man who had three children, but after a period of time she realized the relationship was going nowhere and broke it off. She went back to her parents and took them up on their offer to pay her college expenses. When she found out early in the first semester that she was pregnant, her first thought was "How can this be happening to me?" She felt that her parents and her church would not understand her situation, and she determined that they would never know about it. Yet she knew that she could keep this secret for only a brief period of time. As she began to consider her options, she could only come up with three: to leave her family and try to build a life somewhere else, to have an abortion, or to commit suicide. None was a good option.[20]

Joan's story reminds us that we are faced with some very difficult decisions that can have great consequences. The sixth commandment seems to be very clear: *"You shall not murder"* (Exodus 20:13) offers a moral imperative for today in spite of the fact that many of the issues related to it have become more and more complicated: war, capital punishment, euthanasia, and particularly, abortion!

When we are confronted with these life-and-death issues, a biblical perspective will help us make decisions based on the principles of God's Word and our relationship with Him, not on what is right or wrong as determined by a society which changes its moral stance every time it rains.

In the Hebrew text of this verse there are only two words: the word for "no" and the word for "murder." "No murder." The commandment we learned as children from the King James Version is "Thou shalt not kill." In more recent editions the word "kill" is translated "murder," for certain killings were not prohibited.

Reflected in this commandment are all of the biblical teachings about the sacredness of life. The life of the little baby, the life of the aged parent, the life of the clever person, the life of the simple—all of these lives are

---

[20] Gerald Winslow, *Ministry*, May 1988, page 12ff.

precious. Human life in all of its forms is sacred, created by God, for God's glory. This concept of the sacredness of life is seen in Genesis, the first chapter, when God came on that sixth day to the crown of all of His creation, man and woman. God said He created man and woman in His own image—His own likeness, setting us apart from all other created forms of life.

In Genesis 9:6 we read *"Whoever sheds man's blood, by man his blood shall be shed, for in the image of God He made man."* From these earliest references and on through the New Testament the scripture tells us that life is a gift from God and is holy before the Lord. Therefore, we must not be callous or casual about how we treat lives created in the image and likeness of God.

The problems and tensions of the twenty-first century are such that many young people—even children—are choosing suicide rather than life. I spent time with the family of a teenager who had committed suicide earlier in the day. As I listened to the comments of different members of the family, who were overwhelmed by this tragic loss of their loved one, I wondered, what could have happened? What kind of society have we given teenagers who decide that the best of all options available in a time of stress is taking their own lives? What could we as Christians have done to prevent this tragedy? What could we have done earlier in this teenager's life so that he might understand that life is sacred?

In Midland, we are experiencing an economic boom. There is almost no unemployment and most folks earn higher wages than ever before. We also have a strong community of faith with large churches in multiple denominations. Yet this year there has been an epidemic of youth suicides.

Thomas Aquinas, in interpreting the scripture, said suicide is wrong because it is unnatural, because it is a crime against community, and because it is a usurpation of the power of God.[21] Suicide is wrong because only God is the One who gives and should take life. But let us not despair about the eternal futures of those who have chosen this option. Suicide is wrong—it's not unforgivable. When we stand before the mercy seat of God, His righteousness clothes us, and His sacrifice for our sin covers our wrongdoing.

The biblical imperative against killing sounds simple. Yet is it an admonition that comes quickly to mind when a person is being interviewed for jury duty and the question is posed, "Could you vote in favor of the death penalty?" Does "Thou shall not murder" mean that there should be no death penalty? In the Old Testament capital offenses were listed variously at different times in the Israelites' history: committing murder, engaging in child sacrifice, keeping a dangerous ox, kidnapping, insulting parents, committing incest, practicing idolatry, breaking the Sabbath, and performing witchcraft, among others. The New Testament writings of Paul do not dispute the place of capital punishment in the society of his day (Acts 25:11,

---

21 Barclay, page 77.

Romans 13:4), but the emphasis was a positive one on the preservation of life.

On a radio talk show several ministers were asked "Do you support capital punishment?" I had to answer that in extreme, rare cases I do. Some listeners couldn't reconcile my answer with the concept of the sacredness of life, which I whole-heartedly embrace. I must ask, "What is the way to preserve the life and the rights of the individual to guard against other lives being taken?" Whatever my decision is on capital punishment, I have to ask whether the decision is based, not on public opinion but on my understanding of biblical principles and priority.

Another tough question we must face is "What about war?" Our lively discussions about war show that we have not found a satisfactory answer. I want to be a pacifist. I would like to say that there is no time for war, with the killing of innocents and civilians as well as soldiers. It would be easier to say that war is always wrong, that it is never acceptable.

That position was held by the German Christian, Dietrich Bonhoeffer, who was an extreme pacifist at the beginning of World War II. But as he watched systematic killing of great numbers of people by Hitler, Bonhoeffer finally was forced to consider, "Do I continue to look and try to help bandage the people that the 'mad man' has run over in the street, or would it be more Christian to help take the 'mad man' off the street?" His conscience forced Dietrich Bonhoeffer to become involved in a plot to assassinate

Hitler. When the plot was discovered, Bonhoeffer was arrested and executed in 1945, just before the end of World War II.

Is there such a thing as a "just" war in defense of what is right or in punishment for what is wrong? Aren't there times when individuals and society *must* take a stand against tyranny and oppression and brutality? Can we as Christians sit back saying "Killing is always wrong?" Can we ignore the moral imperative when there is systematic genocide of whole families and races of people? Can we still *not* hurt over the more than 71,000 people who were killed at Hiroshima? When a decision is made to support "justified killing," it is made with a broken heart, with a contrite spirit.

In the last few decades we have heard much about euthanasia. When I hear what Dr. Jack Kevorkian has done it is unbelievable to me that a doctor would be well-known, not for trying to preserve life but by *taking* life. His rationale is that a hurting person with a terminal illness who is in terrible pain should be helped to exit this life as quickly as possible. Our society always tends to take the easy way out. Our attitude is that all of us ought to be immune to pain and that we shouldn't suffer. Yet pain and suffering are a part of life, and many of the greatest teachings of life are those that we have learned when we are hurting and sick.

Many suffering people are far more in tune with the significance of life than the rest of us. I believe that Joni

Eareckson Tada would have committed suicide if she'd had the opportunity. After the accident when she was paralyzed from her neck down, she hoped and prayed to die. If she had had the physical capacity to take her own life, she would have. If Jack Kevorkian had been there, he probably would have been glad to help her commit suicide. And we would have lost Joni Eareckson Tada—the paralyzed Christian who gives her vibrant testimony about what God is doing in her life through her painting as she draws with a brush held in her teeth and as she sings songs of praise and adoration to the Lord. Oh, yes, it's hard—it's been hard—it will *always* be hard for Joni, but should she have given up a life simply because she was hurting?

A related question is "How long do we sustain life through artificial means?" I've stood with many families who have faced this question. Is it possible that we have kept some people out of heaven because we wanted to keep their bodies here on earth? The matter of sustaining unresponsive bodies by mechanical means is best decided by individuals before the fact, when beliefs and convictions can be carefully considered. Both patients and care-givers need the support of family, friends, and church in these situations.

When we consider the sacredness of life, abortion is another important issue we must confront. Is abortion murder or is it not? The answer can be found with the question, "When does life begin?" In the Book of Jeremiah, in the early verses of the first chapter, God said to Jeremiah,

"Before you were formed in your mother's womb, I knew you and sanctified you."

The Psalmist rejoices and praises God saying,

> *"For You formed my inward parts; You wove me in my mother's womb. I will give thanks to You, for I am fearfully and wonderfully made; wonderful are Your works, and my soul knows it very well. My frame was not hidden from You, when I was made in secret, and skillfully wrought in the depths of the earth; Your eyes have seen my unformed substance; and in Your book they were all written the days that were ordained for me, when as yet there was not one of them"* (Psalm 139:13-16).

In the New Testament when Elizabeth, the mother of John the Baptist, was with child; and Mary, the mother of Jesus, walked in, the *"baby leaped in her womb"* (Luke 1:41, 44). The word *baby* there is the same word that the Greeks would use to describe a baby who is breathing and living outside the mother's womb.

So regarding the question, "When does life begin?" I believe that life begins at conception. I cannot find any other answer. If we say that life begins at birth, are we saying that a nine-month-old baby in the womb is not a person? At what week in development does that baby become a person? Who can make that decision?

I visited in the hospital nursery two little boys who were born at twenty-five weeks. When I made a pastoral visit to those little twins in the nursery, I *loved* them. The two little boys each weighed less than two pounds. I don't think I have ever seen another child that small. As small as they were, they were adorable and whole with tiny little feet, tiny little hands, and hair. I prayed for them. Later, when I was praying with their parents, one of the little boys—I believe it was Andrew—took his mother Margaret's finger. His little hand wouldn't even go around her finger, but that little baby, that twenty-five-week-old baby, was squeezing his Mother's hand. When we finished praying and were leaving, she had to pull her hand away from his tiny finger. Those little boys were fighting with all of their inner strength to live. This week I received an announcement of their graduation from high school. They are miracle children.

If that same child was still in his mother's womb, would he not be a person? Driving back to the church from the hospital I saw every person differently because I looked at each one as God's creation. To me they became special, significant. As weird as all of us look—and basically, most of us are ugly!—we are special to God, and life is a gift. How we need to cherish it!

Carol Everett, formerly co-owner of two abortion clinics where thirty-five thousand abortions had taken place, said, "Abortion is not about choice, it's not about rights, it's not even about rape or incest. Abortion is about money."[22] I believe that many doctors who have opted for the easy

---

[22] "Feature of the Week'" *Florida Baptist Witness,* March 18, 1993, page 4.

money in abortions have violated their oaths to preserve life.

Our justice system is curious and inconsistent when it comes to deciding about the sacredness of life. Dr. Abu Hyatt is a New York physician who was arrested because he botched an abortion attempt and the baby was born without an arm. That and some other unrelated incidents caused him to lose his medical license, and he's facing up to sixty-one years in prison because a baby was born without an arm.[23] Ironically, had the procedure been successful, the baby would have been denied life and the doctor could still be practicing medicine.

Paul Jarrett, Jr., M.D., wrote that having seen the horrible social situations and the desperation which drove women to illegal abortions, he decided to perform abortions when they became legal. In 1974 he did twenty-three abortions at Wishard Hospital. He said, "The last abortion I did changed me forever. Instead of a ten-week gestation fetus, the infant I aborted was a fourteen-week pregnancy. After dismembering that fetus, which was too big for the suction curette, I held in my hand the tiny, beating heart and stared in the face of another human being whom I had just murdered. I turned to the scrub nurse and I said, 'I'm sorry.' For four years I had flash-backs to that moment." Only when he accepted Jesus Christ in 1978 was he able to accept forgiveness for those twenty-three deaths.[24]

---

23 AFA Journal, April 1993, page 10.
24 "Abortion in Central Indiana," Metropolitan Baptist Association, Indianapolis, Indiana.

In the United States the most dangerous place for a baby to be is in the mother's womb, for there are more than one and a half million abortions annually.

The story of Joan, whose unexpected pregnancy placed her in a serious dilemma, has not yet been fully played out, but she did not become a part of this statistic. After a great deal of indecision, she opted to carry the child to full term and to put it up for adoption. She was right—her parents and her church were not supportive or accepting, but she received some assistance from a public agency and moved to an apartment. After giving birth she decided to keep her baby, and she and the child have been living alone. She is not enrolled in college, nor is that a prospect.

The conviction that life is sacred should lead us to think about many other issues. If we're consuming more than our share of the world's resources while others are starving, is that murder? If we ignore chemical pollution of the air and water and soil while we are trying to make more money, is that murder?

"Thou shall not murder." The commandment seems so simple when we first read it, but it is very complex when we relate it to the issues of our day. Decisions about these issues should be based on two elements. The first is the element of knowledge. We have not always been informed in our decision-making. We have sometimes been closed to newly discovered truths in God's creation.

In the early 1600s, for example, the young Italian astronomer and physicist Galileo discovered that the sun was the center of the universe. This new discovery was not well received by church officials. A congregation of cardinals, monks and mathematicians examined his work, condemned it as highly dangerous, and summoned him before the tribunal of the Inquisition. In June 1633, Galileo was compelled to go to Rome where he was condemned to renounce the great truths he had discovered and was sentenced to the dungeon of the Inquisition for three years.

More recently, our Baptist forefathers used scripture to justify and support their beliefs that slavery was a part of divine creation.

The second element on which to base our decisions is to establish those basic biblical principles on which our decisions can be made. Belief—no matter how well-intentioned—and truth may not necessarily be the same. Too often we use scripture to validate our beliefs rather than subject our beliefs to scripture for validation of truth.

Our decisions about the sanctity of life—whether abortion, war, suicide, capital punishment, or euthanasia—must be based on biblical principles, not feelings or public opinion. What are some truths of God's Word that enable us to make informed decisions?

The first of these ground-rock principles is that **God is Creator of all life**; *"For from Him and through Him and to Him are all things"* (Romans 11:36). God has created life—not for us—not for society—but for Him. The second biblical principle is that **God is holy and loving**. He will not tolerate sin, but His grace is bestowed upon those who come to Him in repentant faith. I know without a doubt that each of us has taken part in "murder" in some form, wittingly or not, but I believe that God still loves us, as we are assured in the scripture, time after time. A third principle is that **life is sacred,** whether it is in the womb or the nursing home, whether it is healthy or diseased, whether the mind is brilliant or mentally challenged. *All life is a gift of God.*

As Christians we must make decisions in such a way that God will receive glory and that life will be preserved.

Being Moral in an Immoral World

You shall not commit adultery.

Exodus 20:14

Throughout our country there are sweeping changes being made in the way we are looking at moral issues. It is as if a contest is being held for the very soul of our nation.

An estimated one million people came together in Washington, D.C. several years ago representing homosexuals who are fighting for acceptance and legality of their same-sex relationships. On television we saw clergy and government officials endorsing this concept and watching the multi-couple "wedding" ceremony that took place, along with public display of same-sex affection. Even though thirty-two states have passed legislation banning same-sex marriage, the President and Vice President have endorsed the idea. Newsweek had a picture of the President on the cover of its May 21, 2012 edition and hailed him as "The First Gay President."

I believe that the very moral fiber of our nation is being shredded, not just in Washington, D.C. but in communities like the ones we live in.

The Hebrews viewed adultery as a sin both against an individual's body and against society. Society always reflects what is taking place in the family unit. When the family is not intact, then how can society be intact? Further, adultery was ultimately a sin against Yahweh. God has offered the descendants of Abraham the opportunity to live in a covenant relationship with Him so that He might speak through this nation of Israel and others might see what happens to a nation that is in fellowship with the Lord.

In a world where amorality was rampant, Israel was to be the light to the nations. It was to present an alternative to other cultures. Yet the ink was barely dry on its covenant with God when Israel began to act like any of the other nations. There was very little difference between God's people and the people of the world.

The seventh commandment is a very simple statement. As a matter of fact, in the Hebrew text there are only two words—"no adultery." That's all it says. Just as the sixth commandment was "no murder." The seventh commandment was "no adultery." In a very strict Hebrew sense this word refers to the sexual immorality of a married person with someone who is not his or her spouse. This understanding is broadened, though, throughout the Old and New Testaments to describe any sexual activity that is unacceptable to God.

Even though there were clearly articulated standards about sexual immorality, the standards were often breached. Abraham was a man of God, and yet Abraham listened to Sarai his wife and had a sexual relationship with Hagar, her Egyptian maid (Genesis 16). Out of the union came Ishmael, the son of Abraham and Hagar, and through the birth of Ishmael and later Isaac (Abraham and Sarah's son) there came a great division that still separates the people of the world. (See Genesis 17:15 for the story of Sarai's name change).

God didn't tell Abraham to have sex with his wife's handmaiden. Nowhere in the mind and the plan of God was this act acceptable to Him. The cause of the trouble was Abraham and Sarai's attempt to get ahead of God and set up their own plan to have the son which God had promised them.

Great evil resulted from sexual immorality by God's chosen people. King David had a heart for God, but he also had a wandering eye (II Samuel 11). Lust led to adultery, a child was born out of wedlock, a man was killed, and the disastrous situation consumed David and many others of his extended family. Amnon, his son, raped Tamar, his daughter (II Samuel 13:1-19).

Absalom, in defiance of God and his father, committed acts of public immorality with David's concubines (II Samuel

16:20-23). Solomon was given great wisdom, and yet he defied God's teaching and married women from other lands and began to worship their gods (I Kings 11:1-8). The sexual depravity of these individuals in Israel created serious problems in the land.

It is not difficult to trace in the scriptures and throughout history the decay of a nation that loses its moral fiber. Such a nation inevitably becomes second rate or ceases to exist.

The Bible points out the deadly effect of the practice, which some subcultures seem to take for granted, of males seeking sexual fulfillment before or outside of marriage. The seventh chapter of Proverbs graphically portrays the seduction of a young man by a harlot. In verses 22-23 the Wisdom Writer dramatically describes the ultimate price he will pay for following her:

> *Suddenly he follows her,*
> *As an ox goes to the slaughter,*
> *Or as one in fetters to the discipline of a fool,*
> *Until an arrow pierces through his liver;*
> *As a bird hastens to the snare,*
> *So he does not know that it will cost him his life.*

In the earlier verses of the chapter the pleas of a father can be heard. The greatest influence for good or ill in such a situation is the home. Concerned mothers and fathers need to sit down face to face with their children and discuss frankly the right and wrong of the issue. Little good will result, however, if mothers are putting their teenage daughters on birth control pills and if fathers are laughing that "boys will be boys." Parents must hold their children accountable for where they are and what they do and with whom they are associating.

Parents must also teach children that instant gratification and lack of self-discipline can be very dangerous, and parents must set the example. I think it was Augustine who said, "God, give me chastity, but not now!" Many people say, "Lord, I want You to solve this sin in my life, but not yet! I want to live a little bit more."

When the church was born, the dominant world power was the nation of Greece, whose citizens saw nothing wrong in sexual relationships outside of marriage. Demosthenes wrote, "We have mistresses for our pleasure, we have prostitutes for our day-by-day needs, and we have wives to bear our legitimate children and be guardians of our homes."[25]

The Greek religions often included prostitution in the temples. At Corinth in the temple of Aphrodite (the goddess of love) there were a thousand religious prostitutes.[26] As an act of reverence to their god and the miracle of procreation, worshipers would have sexual relationships with male and female priests.

By the time of Jesus the Romans had conquered the Greeks, but the Greeks' immorality had conquered the Romans, and Roman religious practices were little different. The Israelites, however, had the advantage of a long history as

---
25 Barclay, pages 120-121.
26 Barclay, page 123.

God's chosen, punctuated by His direct instructions. Jesus had the advantage of understanding the true significance of these instructions.

In the Sermon on the Mount Jesus outlines a moral maturity that is light-years beyond the Ten Commandments. In speaking about the seventh commandment, he says,

> "You have heard that it was said, 'You shall not commit adultery'; but I say to you that everyone who looks at a woman with lust for her has already committed adultery with her in his heart. If your right eye makes you stumble, tear it out and throw it from you; for it is better for you to lose one of the parts of your body, than for your whole body to be thrown into hell. If your right hand makes you stumble, cut it off and throw it from you; for it is better for you to lose one of the parts of your body, than for your whole body to go into hell.'"
> (Matthew 5:27-30)

The Bible teaches that sex is a gift from God, a gift of intimacy that is to be experienced in the total covenant and commitment of marriage. Marriage is a binding choice; one man, one woman—that is the covenant. Nowhere in the scriptures do we see God encouraging polygamy. God's intention from the very time of creation with Adam and Eve in the Garden of Eden is to build His world around the home created by a man and a woman who are totally and freely committed to each other as companions for life. Anything other than that is unacceptable to God.

Contemporary society continues to try to take the experimentation of the twentieth century and make it the social custom of the twenty-first century. Currently there are several rationalizations for sexual relationship outside of marriage.

A difficult one for Christians is the temptation of *anticipation*.[27] Two Christians fall in love and believe that one day they will be married. They then say, "Well, since we're going to be companions for life and because of our great love for each other, then it's okay for us to become sexually intimate." But it's not okay. It is never okay. Life is uncertain. Many things that we anticipate never come about. If love is that great, then it can enable a couple to wait until the vows are said. How often Christian young people believe sexual relationships outside of marriage seem to be right! When a couple is alone at night on a sofa in a quiet apartment, the decision about how far to go can't be judiciously considered. The understanding about what is right and what is wrong in sexual relationships must be arrived at well ahead of that time and adhered to, regardless of the consequences.

A second scenario we hear about today is the temptation of *experimentation*: a couple needs to live together so that they can see if they're compatible. Now, doesn't that seem reasonable? A lot of what Satan promotes seems reasonable. Unfortunately, couples can no more find out whether there is compatibility in marriage by living together without commitment than a person can find out

---

27 Ideas for the four scenarios come from Barclay pages 148-150.

what it means to grow up in the slums by visiting for a week in the slum area. If there is no commitment to one another, then all one partner has to do when things get tough is to bail out. But when a commitment is made in marriage, the partners must be there and work through those problems that come in human relationships.

Other questions I hear are "Why do we need civil approval?" or "Why do we need religious approval?" or "Why do we need a written contract?" or "Why don't we just consider ourselves married and live together without having anyone else's approval?" The fact is that marriage is at the very *least* a contract between persons, but it is much more than that. At its best, marriage is a promise to God in the presence of witnesses.

A scenario seen less frequently is one in which sincere young women lament that they can't find fulfillment in any other way and who think if they *only had a baby*, then they would have someone to love and nurture. This is especially true within some of the teenage mothers who have not found love at home and long for intimacy they hope will come from a child. That desire becomes a reason for sexual immorality. The Bible teaches us that there are no privileges without responsibility, and the Christian standard is no sex outside of marriage.

An equally difficult moral problem we face in contemporary society is homosexuality. Many persons eager to justify homosexuality in our society refer to societies from a previous age, such as the much-admired cultures of

Greece and Rome, for guidance—or for excuses—as to what is right about homosexuality. Thirteen out of the first fourteen emperors of Rome were practicing homosexuals. The demented Nero had the young boy Sporus castrated, married him in a public ceremony, and claimed him as his spouse. But in spite of all the immorality of the Greek and the Roman societies, homosexuality was never legalized.

Persons eager to justify homosexuality by looking to the classical cultures are quick to point out that Plato advocated homosexuality and talked about the splendor of that kind of love. They neglect to point out that those ideas were expressed in very early writings while in *Laws*, one of the last works that he wrote, the great Plato said (as quoted by Barclay), "The intercourse of men with men, or of women with women is contrary to nature, and the bold attempt was originally due to unbridled lust." Barclay says, "It is one of the most significant facts in this whole matter that the most homosexual society in history regarded it as the act of a madman to legalize homosexuality. The Greek was enslaved by homosexuality, but he knew he was a slave."[28] Those quotations will probably not be seen in the local newspaper or heard on the evening news.

In spite of the attempts of some Christians to justify homosexuality by using the Bible, we find very clearly that the Bible never supports or justifies it but opposes it in no uncertain terms. If God has declared Himself against sexual relations by male and female outside of marriage, how much more could we expect Him to be opposed to

---

28 Barclay, page 159.

sexual relations by persons of the same sex! In Leviticus 18:22 are found these words: *"You shall not lie with a male as one lies with a female; it is an abomination."* That passage earlier lists many other things that are unacceptable, but when it mentions a male lying with a male as with a female, it adds forcefully, *"It is an abomination."*

In Genesis we see that God destroyed the city of Sodom, from which came another word for homosexuality, "sodomize." In Deuteronomy 23:18 there is a statement about homosexuality, which talks about the wages of a dog—referring subtly to the wages that were paid to a male prostitute in the midst of the appearance of religious worship. One of the strongest passages in the Bible condemning homosexuality is in Romans 1:24-28.

> *"Therefore God gave them over in the lusts of their hearts to impurity, so that their bodies would be dishonored among them. For they exchanged the truth of God for a lie, and worshiped and served the creature rather than the Creator, who is blessed forever. Amen. For this reason God gave them over to degrading passions; for their women exchanged the natural function for that which is unnatural, and in the same way also the men abandoned the natural function of the woman and burned in their desire toward one another, men with men committing indecent acts and receiving in their own persons the due penalty of their error. And just as they did not see fit to acknowledge God any longer, God gave them over to a depraved mind, to do those things which are not proper...."*

The most frightening aspect of that chapter is the statement that is used three times: "...*God gave them over*...." As a parent, I know that sometimes children can wear us down and get what they want. They ask and ask and ask, and we say, "No, no, no—yes, get out of my hair!" God says, "No, no, no, no," over and over again. Our Father God does all He can, but if we stubbornly persist, He may no longer stand in our way. The first chapter of Romans says, "*He gave them over to a depraved mind.*" If homosexuality becomes our choice, then we will have to suffer the consequences.

I am not a geneticist; I don't know if homosexuality is in the genes. I do not know if the homosexual proclivity is produced by the environment of the home, if it comes out of the relationship of father and mother and early childhood development. But there are Christian men and women whom I have known who have a penchant for same-sex relationships who abstain from those relationships. In the same way there are those Christians who have a natural tendency toward alcoholism or other habitual sins yet who say, "As a believer I know that this is unacceptable and by the grace of God I will not sin."

I have met with individuals in almost every church I've served who were struggling with the issue of homosexuality. They did not come to their pastor to be condoned. Most of them were really struggling with their sexual identity. They wanted counseling from their pastor and they wanted God to redeem them.

Some people say homosexuality is a problem for which there is no cure. I'll never believe that. In my own counseling ministry I have seen how God can take a homosexual person and turn that life around and use it in a tremendous way. I've seen marriages that were restored when God conquered the sin of homosexuality in the life of a marriage partner.

Another group of homosexuals—the ones who are unashamed of their tendency toward persons of the same sex and are seeking only to celebrate and publicize this proclivity—say, "This is the way I am, and there's nothing wrong with it. It's time that society and the church accepted us and treated us as any other minority!" Homosexuality has absolutely nothing to do with civil rights. It has everything to do with moral parameters. Celebrating one's homosexuality is not the answer to the great moral problem which homosexuality has brought to our world.

There is an increasingly vociferous third group of homosexuals I have encountered. This group is composed of persons who experiment with the gay lifestyle because in sexual perversions they meet an unsatisfied need. They continue to test the boundaries and go beyond them, using as many people as they can for their own personal fulfillment.

What do I believe about these different approaches to the practice of homosexuality? I firmly believe that homosexuality is unacceptable. In all instances I believe that having sex with a person of the same sex is a sin against

God. But I believe that homosexuals are persons of worth and value, created by God for fellowship with Himself, and it is *never* right for us to treat other individuals as less than humans created in the image of God.

There's never a time in our lives when we become immune to sexual temptation. I remember a pastor who was very effective in ministry and who gave every indication of Godliness. He instructed and encouraged me to be faithful in Bible study, scripture memory, and prayer. But he sinned against his wife, against society and the church by committing acts of immorality with a woman not his wife and finally left his wife for this woman. There is an indelible and permanent asterisk by his ministry.

On the other hand, there was Joseph. Before the Law was given—without encouragement of a church, without the accountability of parents, without the support of a group, without the indwelling of the Holy Spirit—Joseph about eighteen years old and in a foreign land, was the object of seduction by a powerful woman. He realized that the rejection of that attempted seduction could be very dangerous, if not fatal. Yet Joseph said "no" to sin and "yes" to God.

Sex is a gift from God that can only be experienced in a fulfilling way in the context of a total commitment of husband and wife. Families must teach this concept through example and through instruction with fathers and mothers clear in their actions and in their teaching.

We, as God's people, must become lovers of God more than lovers of ourselves.

Even if we fail Him, He still loves us. If we confess our sins, He is faithful and just. As He told the woman who was caught in adultery, *"Go and sin no more."* He will meet us where we are and forgive us.

When we become aware of the immorality that surrounds us, let us not lose hope. The church was born into a similarly immoral world. If we rely on God and on biblical teachings, we can live morally in an immoral world.

Taking or Giving?

You shall not steal.

Exodus 20:15

In the story of Naboth's vineyard, Ahab, one of the weakest kings of Israel, wanted Naboth's vineyard, but Naboth wouldn't sell it to him. Ahab's strong, unprincipled wife Jezebel said, "You're the king. Put the man to death and seize the property. I'll show you how." Jezebel's plan was to find two people who would lie for profit, "two worthless men," as the scripture says, two people who would falsely accuse Naboth of treason. When Naboth was executed as a result of the plot, Ahab and Jezebel took possession of the vineyard (I Kings 21:14-16).

This story is about lying and covetousness, and it is also about stealing. Very rarely will a person break the commandments one at a time. To covet another man's money or property may very well mean to *steal* that money or property! There was an old Southern evangelist who used to say, "You don't rob a bank on the spur of the moment. You don't go to bed with someone else's wife or husband on the spur of the moment. That is the end of the process. You rob that bank the moment you start desiring someone else's money!"

One Friday afternoon after playing tennis in Fort Worth, Texas, I discovered my car was stolen. Even though I reported it immediately, I didn't hear anything from the police for several days. When I went with a policewoman to retrieve the car where it had run out of gas, two different people stopped and told us, "I'll tell you who stole your car. He's been driving the car around in this neighborhood for the last several days." They gave us the guy's name and pointed out his house.

A few weeks later I asked the detective who was assigned to the theft, "Did you ever contact that man who stole my car?" He said, "No, we never did. Do you know how many car thefts we have every day in Fort Worth? It would be impossible for us to follow up on all the leads." The terrible truth is that we live at a time when theft is committed so often that it is taken for granted and there is no hope that law enforcement agencies can even begin to cope with it.

Shoplifting, too, is a problem of unbelievable magnitude. Billions of dollars worth of merchandise is stolen every year from stores throughout the country, and the consumer ultimately has to pay for it.

Stealing physical property is just one type of stealing. There are ways to take what belongs to another person other than by breaking into a house or taking a pistol into a convenience store to rob the cashier. Some steal by not paying their debts. Some steal by falsifying income tax returns. One man wrote a letter to the IRS: "I haven't been able to sleep for weeks. I lied on my tax return and I have a guilty conscience. Enclosed is a check for $100. If that doesn't clear up my conscience, I'll send you the rest."

That anecdote is amusing, but unfortunately many of us think, if I can get by with it, then its okay. The person who discovers that the cashier made a mistake in his favor thinks, the store's mistake is my good fortune!

The year Hurricane Andrew devastated a part of Florida, price-gougers rushed into the area as soon as the roads were clear. These scoundrels were overpricing essential material and repairs to profit from someone else's loss. The kind of theft is just as reprehensible as was the looting that occurred in the aftermath of the hurricane. Stealing from others, even in such a subtle manner, is a violation of the eighth commandment.

Immediately after a severe hailstorm in the Fort Worth area where we lived, many of our neighbors would get new roofs, whether their roof had suffered major damage or not. The rationale was, why worry about it since the insurance company was going to pay for it. I wonder how those folks who stole their new roofs could miss the fact that ultimately they, and the rest of us, would pay increased premiums as a result of the fraudulent claims.

Theft frequently occurs in the workplace, and the guilty parties are often the employees. When I was in high school, I worked in a grocery store. If I found my parents shopping at any other grocery store than *our* grocery store, they were in trouble with me, for I was extremely loyal. I watched with embarrassment and shame as I gradually learned about the number of my fellow workers who were cheating the company by taking extended coffee breaks, eating fruit they didn't pay for, or even shoplifting.

But it works two ways. Employers also steal from employees. Do you know how many retiring employees have no savings to retire on because unscrupulous money handlers have robbed their pension funds? Are you aware of the many itinerant farm workers across the nation, some in our own area, who work at hard labor and are robbed of a decent wage? The admonition in Deuteronomy 24:14 is, "*You shall not oppress a hired servant who is poor and needy, whether he is one of your countrymen or one of your aliens who is in your land in your towns.*" James 5:4 says "*Behold, the pay of the laborers who mowed your fields, and which has been withheld by you, cries out against you; and the outcry of those who did the harvesting has reached the ears of the Lord of Sabaoth.*"

When I was pastor of First Baptist Church in Gonzalez, Texas, we learned that a theft had taken place at the church. Money was missing from the office. We never learned the identity of the thief. The membership was shocked that anyone would steal from the church.

I wrote an article in our weekly newsletter using the event as a teaching tool, stating that we had learned that this theft from our church was not an isolated incident. Other robberies had taken place. The situation was complicated by the fact that these other thieves had been identified as members of the church and some of them held positions of leadership. Should we press charges? I continued by writing that, unlike the theft from the office, these other robberies were the results of withholding tithes and offerings. I added Malachi 3:8-10 to the newsletter:

> *"'Will a man rob God? Yet you are robbing Me! But you say, 'How have we robbed You?' 'In tithes and offerings. You are cursed with a curse, for you are robbing Me, the whole nation of you! Bring the whole tithe into the storehouse, so that there may be food in My house, and test Me now in this,' says the Lord of hosts, 'if I will not open for you the windows of heaven, and pour out for you a blessing until it overflows.'"*

A large number of people try to justify the fact they do not tithe the required ten percent. Some say, "I don't like the way the church is spending the money." Does God say a tenth is the Lord's if we like the way the church business is carried on? "We'll tithe when there's a building fund we just don't tithe when there's a mission trip." A Christian doesn't sit down every month and decide what he is going to do with the tithe or whether he is going to give the tithe or not. Either he gives the Lord His tithe or he steals God's tithe from Him. The Bible is clear: to take the tithe and use it to pay bills or to go to Acapulco on vacation or to buy a certificate of deposit is to steal from God.

Some folks say, "Oh, the tithe is an Old Testament law. God gave them that requirement to finance the temple." The truth is that long before there was a temple, the book of Genesis tells us, there were tithes. Abraham tithed to Melchizedek, king of Salem, a priest of God Most High (Genesis 14:20) before Israel was a nation, before there was a tabernacle or before there was a Levitical priesthood to support. Christians believe that property belongs to God. When we bring our tithes and offerings to the Lord, we're saying, "Lord, not only is a tenth Yours; all heaven and earth are Yours. I am Yours." When we tithe, we simply acknowledge the fact that all is the Lord's.

We may know in our hearts that we've broken the eighth commandment: by stealing from stores, by stealing in the work place, by stealing at church, or by any one of a hundred different ways that we can steal. If so, what must we do with such knowledge? The biblical example is to repent and make restitution.

Zaccheus was a tax collector who had defrauded many people. When Jesus came into his house and into his heart, Zaccheus became a changed person. He was made so new that he said he was going to give half of his possessions to the poor and restore fourfold to the people he had taken money from. Jesus didn't tell him to do those things (Luke

19:1-10). He volunteered because he had been saved. He was familiar with the law of the sheep in Exodus 22:1—if you take a man's sheep, then you are to restore that sheep fourfold.

The Apostle Paul, in instructing the Ephesians about the life worthy of the Christian, mentions stealing specifically: *"He who steals must steal no longer; but rather he must labor, performing with his own hands what is good, so that he will have something to share with one who has need"* (Ephesians 4:28). The Christian life is much more than just keeping the commandments. To refrain from stealing is not enough. Jesus tells us that life comes in giving of ourselves to others. In the Sermon on the Mount Jesus talked about going the extra mile, about giving to him who asks of you, about not turning away from him who wants to borrow from you. Jesus is concerned that we not take from others but, more than that, he wants us to share that which we hold in stewardship.

Paul, in writing to the Romans about the commandments, concludes by saying that *"Love does no wrong to a neighbor* (13:10)." He admonishes the people to pay up their commitments so that one owes *"nothing to anyone except to love one another"* (13:8).

Fortunately, the same events which bring out the worst in some people bring out the best in others. While price-gougers rushed to South Florida following Hurricane Andrew, so did many Christians from across the country to help where they could, working with their hands or offering other services, motivated by love. This kind of outpouring is the response Christians make to calamities wherever they occur. Why should this be so? Because Christians have learned that we can keep the ancient laws and still not experience the fulfilling life. Joy comes, not in just refraining from breaking the commandments but in doing good.

Speaking the Truth in Love

You shall not bear false witness against your neighbor.

Exodus 20:16

While I was living in Virginia I had the privilege of being part of a support group. Eight of us met throughout the year to encourage one another and to hold each other accountable. All of us were in the ministry and most of them were known throughout Virginia Baptists. The first time I met with them we met for a two day retreat at our church's retreat center (Columbia Baptist Church of Falls Church). I was astounded at their honesty with one another. It was the second day when I told my story and I began by saying that I wanted to confess a sin I had never confessed before. I told them it was a burden for me and something that left me without control. I said, "I can't keep confidences."

This went over really well after they had all told their secrets and especially since I was the new guy. Of course I was joking! But "bearing false witness against a neighbor" is a serious concern. We may be guiltier of violating the ninth commandment than any of the other laws and yet counselors seldom have someone who comes and says "Help me. I'm breaking the ninth commandment."

When given from Mount Sinai, this commandment was a direct reference to a practice being used in the law courts of the day when a person was brought into court to testify against another. We know from the scripture that under the Law two eyewitnesses were necessary for conviction.

> *"A single witness shall not rise up against a man on account of any iniquity or any sin which he has committed; on the evidence of two or three witnesses a matter shall be confirmed. If a malicious witness rises up against a man to accuse him of wrongdoing, then both the men who have the dispute shall stand before the Lord, before the priests and the judges who will be in office in those days. The judges shall investigate thoroughly; and if the witness is a false witness and he has accused his brother falsely, then you shall do to him just as he had intended to do to his brother. Thus you shall purge the evil from among you"* (Deuteronomy 19:15-19).

We can understand the seriousness with which lying in court was viewed since one who gave false testimony was subject to the same penalty demanded for the person he was accusing. Several stories in the scripture indicate that such use of false witnesses did occur. The story about Naboth's vineyard (1 Kings 21) reached its climax when Jezebel arranged for "two worthless men" to accuse Naboth of treason.

Much later, when the disciples were struggling to be obedient to the faith, Stephen, who was "doing wonderful things among the people," was brought up before the council of priests by false accusers who said, "*We have heard him speak blasphemous words against Moses and against God* (Acts 6:11)." Stephen's tragic death was a direct result of their deliberate action of false accusation.

Numerous other references make us aware that the ninth commandment has a much broader application than bearing false witness in a court. All the prophets exhort against rampant lying among the people. References are to be found in Hosea, Isaiah, Jeremiah, Malachi, and Ezekiel. Both Psalms and Proverbs are filled with examples of sins and consequences of lying. One section in Proverbs lists seven specific actions that are abominable to the Lord. Of the seven, three are sins of speech: "*a lying tongue, a false witness who breathes out lies and one who spreads strife among brothers*" (Proverbs 6:16-19).

The ninth commandment is not just a relic of the past. It is valuable and necessary today because deception is a part of daily life as it was in the world of the ancient Hebrews. Mark Twain is reported to have said that there are eight hundred and sixty-nine ways to lie. Some of us may have invented additional ways!

William Barclay's list is not that long, but it makes us aware that much of the lying we do is subtle and perhaps unrecognized as a transgression.[29] For example, the person who enjoys gossip and passes it on is a liar. The person who fabricates to avoid unpleasant situations or unwarranted consequences is also a liar.

This practice we may have learned when we were very young because we were afraid to tell the truth after we had disobeyed our parents. The *Family Circus* cartoon often illustrates the children's denials. While the broken lamp lies shattered on the floor, the kids all say, "Not me!" "Not me!" and the phantom labeled NOT ME hovers near. Early in life many of us learn not to own up to our actions.

Fabrication is part of our folk lore in Texas. The story is told that George Washington was actually born in Texas. When he was young his father came to him and asked "Who chopped down the cottonwood tree?" Young George answered, "I cannot tell a lie. I did." His dad said "If you cannot tell a lie then we cannot stay in Texas," so they moved to Virginia.

Most children go through a period when they have difficulty distinguishing what is true from what is fiction. When they begin to exaggerate the truth or build fantasies on a basis of truth, we need to bring them back and discuss what actually happened or the reality of the situation. Too many children will carry this habit of childhood lying into adult years.

---

29 William Barclay, pages 189-193.

Some of us develop a habit of boasting in which we tell not what really happened but what we would have liked to have happened. We project those things which we wish we had said or done into the telling. We exaggerate or totally fabricate experiences about our past. Some may only wish they were the athletes they proclaim they used to be. One fisherman admitted that a fish is the only animal that continues to grow even after it has died. This is telling a lie.

There are also lies for profits. In addition to the obvious examples found in false advertising of products, insider trading in the stock market, and the like, instances of the journalistic lie have enriched numerous perpetrators. One glaring example is Janet Cooke, the reporter for *The Washington Post,* who fabricated a series of stories about an eight-year-old heroin addict, which won a Pulitzer Prize. She later was forced to return the prize and was fired from her job. Other examples can be found in abundance in the tabloid racks at the checkout counter in any grocery store.

Blogging and electronic communication have provided an easy forum for perpetrating half-truths and lies. The church community has been no exception. Some bloggers write stories about religious leaders or institutions based on assumptions or even nothing more than their own imaginations and present them as proven facts. Countless lives and ministries have been damaged by these vicious fabrications. I cannot imagine the consequences for individuals who pretend to be ministers while slandering the Bride of Christ.

Calling it the lie of silence, Barclay points out that there are times when we can lie without even opening our mouths.[30] We should speak the truth, but because we are afraid we often remain silent. Where was Mary Magdalene when the crowd was crying, "Crucify him!"? Where was Lazarus during that dangerous time? Jesus raised him from the dead just a few days earlier, yet when near his own home town of Bethany the crowd was yelling, "Crucify him, crucify him!" Lazarus' voice was not heard. The contemporary situations in which you and I fail to speak up may be neither as dramatic nor as frightening, but we nevertheless bear the responsibility for speaking out in defense of right. The lie of silence is the coward's refuge.

So is the lie of half-truth, often born of carelessness but at other times of malice. At Jesus' trial before Caiaphas, a false witness said, *"This man stated, 'I am able to destroy the temple of God and to rebuild it in three days'"* (Matthew 26:61). That was a truthful statement, yet Jesus was referring to the temple of His body, not Herod's temple (John 2:21). The events that followed Jesus' trial can be partly blamed on this half-truth. The lie of the half-truth is often more dangerous than an out-and-out falsehood.

One of the most hurtful lies is the lie to self. People who deceive themselves never learn who they really are. They develop a false sense of identity because they have never come face to face with the truth about themselves. Lying to one's self is a sin against personality. It's a sin against family. It's a sin against society. A friend recently

---

30 Barclay, page 191.

reminded me of the impressive statement made by former President Gerald Ford shortly after the Richard Nixon resignation: "Truth," said President Ford "is the glue that holds society together." His statement reminds us that *community* depends on *truthfulness*.

The Apostle Paul said as much to the church in Ephesus: *"Therefore, laying aside falsehood, speak truth each one of you with his neighbor, for we are members of one another"* (Ephesians 4:25). It is not difficult to realize that telling the truth or the opposite lying, is basic in both our individual and corporate relationships.

Perhaps the most incredible lie is the lie to God. I heard a story about an alcoholic who really struggled with his drinking problem. His godly wife tried everything she could to encourage him. After a period of sobriety, one night he came home drunk once again. His despairing wife took him by the arm and dragged him to his knees beside her and prayed, "Lord, my husband is drunk again." At this time he stumbled to his feet and said, "Don't tell God!" William Barclay says that"...it is obvious folly to try to deceive Him who searches the hearts of men and who knows our thoughts as well as he hears our words and sees our deeds."[31]

The ninth commandment and all the subsequent biblical references to it attest to the human difficulty in controlling one's tongue. James notes that a simple bit in the mouth of a powerful horse and a small rudder can guide a huge

---
31 Barclay, page 193.

ship. In the same way, this small member, the tongue, can drive the much larger body of which it is a part (James 3:3-5). It has the power to direct our lives and shape us and determine our effectiveness or ineffectiveness.

James also compares the tongue to a fire. A very small flame can set an entire forest on fire (3:5). A tongue can utter just a small word and do infinite damage. A word has life beyond its utterance, and the damage it does may be out of proportion to its size.

A story is told of a woman who had a wicked tongue. "She often spread malicious gossip and invariably was sorry for having done so. Eager to make restitution, she sought out a judicious friend for advice. The wise person took her to a high hill on a windy day, gave her a pillow filled with feathers, and told her to cut the pillow open and shake all the feathers out. The wind began to blow them in all different directions. 'Now,' he said, 'go pick up all the feathers and put them back in the pillow and you'll be forgiven.' 'That's impossible,' she said. 'The wind has blown them far away so that I could never find them all.' 'Ah,' he said, 'in the same way you can never recover the impact of your malicious words.'"

How is it possible to tame the tongue? We can learn to speak the truth by seeking the truth. The New Testament is full of encouragement to do so. Jesus himself promised *"...and you will know the truth, and the truth will make you free"* (John 8:32).

Paul's advice to the Ephesians can be just as powerful for us: *"Let no unwholesome word proceed from your mouth, but only such a word as is good for edification according to the need of the moment, so that it may give grace to those who hear"* (Ephesians 4:29).

As believers we can be intentional about telling the truth. We can become sensitive to the times when our tongues assume control of our better judgment. The Holy Spirit lives within us to do what we cannot do for ourselves.

Desiring the Best

You shall not covet your neighbor's house; you shall not covet your neighbor's wife or his male servant or his female servant or his ox or his donkey or anything that belongs to your neighbor.

Exodus 20:17

I am fortunate to live in a relatively nice neighborhood. All the houses are comfortable. Why should I covet my neighbor's house? I love my wife. Why should I covet my neighbor's wife? To my knowledge none of my neighbors have slaves; actually one does have a yard man that would sure come in handy! Maybe the tenth commandment has more to say to me than I first thought.

Why does the list in the scripture place *house* before *wife* and then fail to mention *children* at all? Is this an indication of some kind of priority? Unfortunately the English translation allows us to misread this text. *House* is an inadequate word for the Hebrew *beth,* which means more than the structure where we live. In the Old Testament context *house* is more accurately *household,* including a man's whole family and entire property. The same word is used in the Genesis story of Noah. When God instructed Noah to take his *beth* with him into the ark, he obviously did not mean to take a dwelling structure but all the people and provisions for which he bore responsibility. The general maxim of the tenth commandment then, is all-encompassing: You shall not covet *anything* that belongs to your neighbor.

In the New Testament Greek there are two words that are used interchangeably with "covet." One is the word for "more" and conveys the idea that "more" is never enough. It is often translated "greed." It conveys the idea of "receiving from avarice" and calls up a picture of someone trying to fill up a purse that has no bottom in it or trying to satisfy a thirst that can never be quenched.

The other word that is translated "covet" means "reaching out for forbidden fruit." In his *"Confessions"* Saint Augustine illustrates this usage when he tells about a boyhood neighbor's pear tree that was heavy with fairly ordinary fruit. As a matter of fact, his family had pear trees in their own yard. But one night he and his friends went into the neighbor's yard and stole the neighbor's pears. They ate some of them but most of them they just threw to the pigs. Later he reflected, "Why did I steal my neighbor's pears? The only reason I took those pears was that there was a kind of joy about that which was forbidden, and if I did what was forbidden I would find pleasure in that action itself."[32]

The picture from both of these meanings for *covet* is that human nature, in general, can't be satisfied. We've got to have more and more and more...but more is never enough. The scriptures point out again and again that this sin of greed is often the foundation of other sins. In the very beginning God provided everything that Eve and Adam needed. Yet when the serpent showed Eve the fruit of the forbidden tree and she realized that it was desirable, she ate, and sin and death entered the world.

After Joshua led the Israelites into the Promised Land, God gave them victory in battle at Jericho. Before that battle God told Joshua and the people that they were not to take bounty from Jericho, for all the treasures were to go into the treasury of the Lord (Joshua 6:19). However, Achan, one of the soldiers, could not resist the temptation of beautiful things, specifically a mantle from Shinar, two hundred shekels of silver and a gold bar that weighed fifty shekels. "*And I saw them. I coveted them. And I took them*" (Joshua 7:21).

Because of this sin of covetousness, God caused the army of Israel to be defeated by the much smaller force of Ai. When his sin was discovered, Achan and his entire household were killed because he had disobeyed the Lord. "*And all Israel stoned them with stones; and they burned them with fire after they had stoned them with stones*" (Joshua 7:25).

---

32 Barclay, page 195.

Paul implored the Colossians to set their minds on the things that are above and not on the things that are on the earth (Colossians 3:2). In listing the undesirable habits to be cast off, he rates covetousness alongside of fornication and calls it "idolatry "(Colossians 3:5). The attitude of the present-day consumer culture in Western society might well be termed idolatrous. What else can it be called when our lives are controlled by the desire for more than we can ever use?

In the sixties when college students were interviewed about their life goals they often mentioned ideas that were very different from their parents. Many of the goals were lofty and related to some aspect of improving society. Today it appears that the goals are more materialistic rather than altruistic. The idea is to get a job that helps you make a lot of money. In my opinion a few decades ago more students in college studied science, to explore God's creation to understand how to grow more food or construct a cheaper energy source. Some studied psychology to find how people can live in a more harmonious and healthy way.

I hear of doctors who entered their professions to help hurting people; yet attend medical conferences where much of the discussion centers on protecting wealth. Ministers are not exempt from the same greed and entitlements of other professions. Sports are dominated with multimillion dollar salaries. Teams exploit players and players make unrealistic demands just to play a game. Bobby Jones, one of the greatest golfers ever, never played for money or endorsed products for money. He is reported to have said that one day money will ruin sports. These words have proven prophetic.

A story attributed to Tolstoy is about a poor man who was promised all the land he could walk around in one day. Early one morning the man began to walk as hard as he could. He pushed himself beyond his physical limitations. Near the end of the day when he had almost circled the large area of land he would soon acquire, he dropped dead.[33] Many of us spend all of life trying to collect all the possessions we can acquire. Finally when we have circled them, we drop dead. In the parable of the fool the death angel says, *"Now who will own what you have prepared?"* (Luke 12:20)

A sociologist who did a study that involved fifty people over the age of ninety-five asked the question, "If you had your life to live over again, what would you do differently?" Three answers came through most often:

- I would take more time to reflect.
- I would take more risks.
- I would do more things that would live on after I die.[34]

We don't have to wait until we are ninety-five to understand that the meaningful and lasting qualities of life do not include the accumulation of things. Whether we are seventy or seventeen, we can learn the wisdom

[33] John Bisagno, *Positive Obedience*, Zondervan, 1979, page 73.
[34] Tony Campolo, *Who Switched the Price Tags*, Word Books, 1986, page 29.

acquired by these folks who learned from over ninety years of life experience.

The use of the word *covet* implies something that is negative. Indeed, to this point, we have consistently used it as such. It is essentially a neutral word, however, with its connotation coming from the context in which it is used. It means "to desire" or "to wish for eagerly." If we desire inappropriately, then it is obviously negative. If we wish eagerly for something appropriate, then it is just as obviously positive.

The commandment reads, *"Thou shall not covet…,"* yet we must look beyond the concept of refraining from coveting our neighbor's belongings. We must go one step farther; we must desire what is good and right. We must learn to be content in whatever our circumstances. *"Make sure that your character is free from the love of money, being content with what you have; for He Himself has said, 'I will never desert you, nor will I ever forsake you"* (Hebrews 13:5). Paul said,

> *"I have learned to be content in whatever circumstances I am. I know how to get along with humble means, and I also know who to live in prosperity; in any and every circumstance I have learned the secret of being filled and going hungry, both of having abundance and suffering need"* (Philippians 4:11-12).

After Paul describes the gifts that seem dramatic—healing, prophecy, tongues, and miracles—he adds, *"…but earnestly desire the greater gifts."* And what is the greater gift? The greater gift is *love* (1 Corinthians 12:31-13:1). Jesus affirmed to us that satisfaction comes when we learn to love God with heart and soul and mind and strength, and love others as we love ourselves (Mark 12:29-31). In the Sermon on the Mount Jesus said that those who hunger and thirst for righteousness will be satisfied (Matthew 5:6).

Many centuries after God gave the commandment Paul speaks of its value for Christians. In trying to explain the purpose of the Law as it should be applied in the lives of the Roman Christians, he refutes the notion that the ancient Law was no longer holy and just and good. After all, he said, *"For I would not have known about coveting if the Law had not said, 'You shall not covet'"* (Romans 7:7). The recognition of the sin is the very first step on the road to repentance. And the desire for cleansing hastens us down the road to redemption.

Epilogue

I heard a story that early in his career Dr. Charlie Shedd, the author and minister, gave a series of lectures on parenting. He delivered his lectures which he called "The Ten Commandments for Parents," all over the nation to large crowds. After he and his wife Martha had their firstborn, he changed the name of his lectures to "Ten Hints for Parents" and enjoyed continued success. Then he and Martha had another child. He writes that he renamed the lecture series once more: "A Few Tentative Suggestions for Parents." When they had the third child, he quit giving the lectures.

The anecdote illustrates very well a truism I've observed about life. We tend to have absolutes in our lives when we are unaware of the issues! Then, when we are confronted by real issues, we abandon the absolutes!

Real issues are confronting us on every side, literally bombarding us through the media and in our personal situations. Everything nailed down is coming loose! We have some who are saying there are no absolutes (which is itself an absolute statement). Everything is relative. Truth is whatever appears right in a person's mind. However this is not the time to abandon the absolutes. In fact, now is the time to embrace these principles embodied in the Ten Commandments.

First, we must recognize that the giving of the Ten Commandments was not an exercise in restrictive power by the God of the universe. God was not putting boundaries on individuals so that He could bind them up in a legalism that would preclude all opportunities for joy and fulfillment. In spite of the fact that most of these commandments are in the form of prohibitions, they provide a positive moral parameter within which we can find freedom and celebrate life.

The commandments provide the moral guidance for living in the larger community. The symbol of the Ten Commandments can be seen in several places in the Supreme Court Building in Washington, D. C. This is a reminder that the Ten Commandments form the basis of all laws in our society.

The commandments also speak to the ways in which we can establish and strengthen vital relationships. The first four deal with humanity's connection to God. If our relationship to God is right, then that with other persons comes more easily and naturally. The last six commandments spell out how people should be valued and how we should treat one another.

Yet the commandments within themselves are incomplete. When Jesus spoke the Sermon on the Mount, He said *"For I say to you that unless your righteousness surpasses that of the scribes and Pharisees, you will not enter the kingdom of heaven"* (Matthew 5:20). There may have been no group of people historically who kept the Ten Commandments better than the Pharisees. They made it their vocation to obey the Law. However, as disciplined and sincere as they were, it was not enough. They too were law breakers. They too needed a new nature.

The primary purpose of the commandments was to point the generations to Christ (Galatians 3:24). Today, after the event of Christ's resurrection, we have a unique and privileged view of God's loving action. In this covenant God furnished a mirror that reflects our need for redemption. Just as a mirror shows me my condition and what I need to do to make myself presentable to others, so the mirror of the Ten Commandments shows me what I must do to be presentable for God.

The mirror will not make me perfect and neither can the Law (Hebrews 7:19). Yet what the Law cannot do Jesus can. Just as God wrote the Law on stone, so Jesus Christ writes it on our hearts.

During a sermon on the Ten Commandments, the preacher asked a small boy "Is it wrong to kill?"

The boy said, "Yes sir, it's wrong to kill."

"Which commandment is that?"

"That's the fifth commandment."

"Well," asked the preacher "is it wrong to steal?"

"Yes sir, it's wrong to steal."

"Which commandment is that?"

The boy responded, "It is commandment number seven."

The preacher asked, "Is it wrong to pull a cow's tail?"

This question was getting into deep theology for the boy, but after some thought he replied, "Yes sir, it's wrong to pull a cow's tail."

"What commandment is that?" asked the amused preacher.

The boy stammered, "I think it is number eleven, but we haven't gotten to it yet. I know it starts something like 'What God has joined together…'"

We find reflections of the Ten Commandments throughout the New Testament. Instinctively they are also written on the human heart. Yet even though there may be an awareness of what is right and what is wrong we all have found that we come up short. We need a new nature. We need the grace of a holy God.

In a world where everything nailed down is coming loose, the Ten Commandments still stand as God's Law for the human race. Jesus has come to write those laws upon our heart so that we can live in harmony with Him and others.

"For He rescued us from the domain of darkness, and transferred us to the kingdom of His beloved Son, in whom we have redemption, the forgiveness of sins" (Colossians 1:13-14).

CPSIA information can be obtained at www.ICGtesting.com
Printed in the USA
LVOW130056210612

287022LV00001B/8/P

9 780985 326333